AFFIRMING RELIGIOUS FREEDOM

AFFIRMING RELIGIOUS FREEDOM

HOW VATICAN COUNCIL II
DEVELOPED THE CHURCH'S TEACHING
TO MEET TODAY'S NEEDS

KENNETH D. WHITEHEAD

ST PAULS

Library of Congress Cataloging-in-Publication Data

Whitehead, K.D.
  Affirming religious freedom : how Vatican Council II developed the church's
teachings to meet today's needs / by Kenneth D. Whitehead.
    p. cm.
  Includes bibliographical references (p.) and index.
  ISBN-13: 978-0-8189-1313-6 (alk. paper)
  ISBN-10: 0-8189-1313-4 (alk. paper)
  1. Vatican Council (2nd : 1962-1965). Declaratio de libertate religiosa. 2. Freedom
of religion. 3. Catholic Church—Doctrines.   I. Vatican Council (2nd : 1962-1965).
Declaratio de libertate religiosa. English.   II. Title.
  BX8301962.A45 D4838   2010
  261.7'2—dc22

                          2009050688

Produced and designed in the United States of America by the
Fathers and Brothers of the Society of St. Paul,
2187 Victory Boulevard, Staten Island, New York 10314-6603
as part of their communications apostolate.

ISBN 10: 0-8189-1313-4
ISBN 13: 978-0-8189-1313-6

Printing Information:

Current Printing - first digit   1   2   3   4   5   6   7   8   9   10

Year of Current Printing - first year shown

2010   2011   2012   2013   2014   2015   2016   2017   2018   2019

CONTENTS

A NEW EMPHASIS ON RELIGIOUS FREEDOM

EVER SINCE 9/11, 2001, the world has been particularly confronted with the acute moral, political and practical problem of how some who believe themselves to be in possession of religious truth also believe themselves to be able to impose that truth on others by coercion and even by force and violence. It is a problem that has necessarily engaged governments responsible for the safety and protection of their peoples. They are obliged to try to find appropriate and measured responses to terrorists motivated by a religiously based ideology that claims religious sanction for indiscriminate attacks on innocent people, including women and children. According to this "jihadist" way of thinking all "infidels" anywhere, apparently, are potential targets.

Related to this contemporary jihadist terrorist phenomenon is the apparently even much more widespread belief among the adherents of some religions, non-Christian for the most part today, to the effect that force and violence, or, at the very least state-backed discrimination, are legitimate means to advance a cause declared to be religious. This belief often takes the form of overt discrimination, or even violence, against Christian minorities in their countries. This kind of religious coercion or discrimination is much more common than the jihadist or terrorist kind, of course, and it certainly does occur quite widely, both historically and in various parts of the world today. The unhappy fact that it does continue to occur today cannot be anything but very serious and troubling.

It should not be any surprise, therefore, that both the jihadist and the anti-Christian types of coercion and religious discrimination have not failed to get the attention of the Catholic Church and her top leadership. Pope Benedict XVI in particular, like his predecessor, Pope John Paul II, has spoken out on more than one occasion on religiously motivated violence and discrimination in general — especially when directed against Christians — and on terrorism in particular. For example, in his address on January 8, 2009 to the Vatican diplomatic corps — sometimes called his "State of the World" address — the pope deplored "terrorist attacks that have sown death and destruction in countries like Afghanistan, India, Pakistan, and Algeria." Moreover, the pope continued, "acts of discrimination, and the very grave attacks directed at thousands of Christians in the past year show to what extent it is not material poverty, but also moral poverty that damages peace."

Pope Benedict further pointed out that communities living in Asia, for example, "are often numerically small, yet they wish to contribute, in a convincing and effective way, to the common good, stability, and the progress of their countries as they bear witness to the primacy of God, which sets up a healthy order of values and grants a freedom more powerful than acts of injustice…. The Church, as has often been said, does not demand privileges but the full application of the principles of religious freedom…"

Religious freedom. Or religious liberty. We shall use these terms interchangeably, as is pretty much the custom today. Both terms denote a subject that the Pope has necessarily had to bring up and talk about. In his "State of the World" address to the cardinals the year before, in fact, the Pope had found it necessary to address the very same subject. And yet again on that same subject, on December 5, 2005, the Holy Father commemorated the fortieth anniversary of the issuance by the Second Vatican Council of its Declaration on Religious Freedom, *Dignitatis Humanae.* He praised this conciliar document, which had declared religious freedom to be a right that accrues to every human person by virtue of that person's human dignity, a right that also must be accorded to every human community as well.

Affirming religious freedom today, however, has not always gotten an entirely favorable response. As many will remember, the international controversy that was stirred up by the lecture that Pope Benedict delivered at Regensburg University in September, 2006, went far beyond what anybody would have imagined could result from an academic lecture. For the pope's Regensburg Lecture was primarily concerned with the topic of faith and reason, and the need to employ the latter in the service of the former. However, the pope's mention and citation of a saying of a fourteenth-century Byzantine emperor, who had stigmatized what he called the Prophet Muhammad's "command to spread by the sword the faith he preached," caused a worldwide furor among Muslims, including some violent demonstrations, some of the repercussions of which are echoing still — although one of the positive consequences of this whole affair was to set in motion an ongoing Vatican dialogue with some Muslim leaders on the subject of religious freedom among other topics.

Religious freedom thus continues to be a relevant contemporary topic: how *can* tolerance and accommodation be fostered, and strife and conflict and persecution avoided, when rival claims to religious truth seem to require adherents of a given religion to demand compliance with their believed truth and hence to feel justified in resorting to force to see that their particular religious viewpoint should prevail? If religious truth is God's truth, then it surely *must* apply to everybody; and everybody must therefore also accede to it, even if compulsion is required to bring that about. So goes the logic — an all too familiar way of thinking! This logic is quite clear, in fact. Nor is any extensive or profound knowledge of history necessary to recall a time when Christians too, Catholics, Protestants, and Orthodox alike, found this same logic compelling. Not only did they not always forgo various forms of pressure or compulsion to promote their respective versions of what they thought the propagation of Christ's glad tidings required; they sometimes considered it a solemn duty to do so, at least in some circumstances.

A medieval Christian emperor such as Charlemagne, for example, required as a matter of course the conversion to Catholic Christianity of those he conquered by the sword. A "Most Christian" king such as Louis XIV of France similarly pursued a policy of religious unity on the part of those under, or who came under, his sway. This was the *typical* stance of a Christian monarch, in fact, in the era of monarchies. Everyone is also surely pretty much aware, for example, of how those who opposed the religious settlement of King Henry VIII of England and his successors generally fared: a substantial number of them became martyrs. Nor were the citizens of John Calvin's Geneva allowed any choice in the matter of whether they were going to profess the Calvinist version of the Christian faith or not; the Christian princes who imposed Lutheranism followed the same policies. Nor does it seem that things were much different in the states ruled by the Eastern Orthodox emperors and other rulers. And all of these cases of coercion by Christians are merely illustrative examples of a long and sad history.

Compulsion in religious belief and practice was certainly the accepted thing during the religious wars following the Protestant Reformation and the Catholic Reform of the sixteenth and seventeenth centuries. The policy of *cuius regio, eius religio* ["whoever rules, his religion"] was the way in which religious conflicts within Christendom ultimately got settled by the Peace of Augsburg (1555) and later by the Peace of Westphalia (1648).

Rulers dictated what the religion of their people would be in the territories they controlled, and within those territories there were few or no compunctions about using the power of the state to require religious conformity. Nor did the fact that the effort to impose religious conformity did not always succeed often seem to discourage those who practiced it. It was the accepted practice, including in the first English colonies of what eventually became the United States, where Catholic Maryland's original experiment in religious toleration was abolished as soon as there were enough "democratic" Protestant votes to bring that about. There was simply no general idea around in those days that tolerance and religious freedom ought to prevail.

How did it come about, then, that we now have a pope extolling religious freedom and calling for its application in situations today where it is not being respected? How did the once near universally accepted practice of compulsion get changed? Actually, there has been a rather long development within the Christian world where sad experience eventually did teach those on all sides that trying to force what was sincerely believed to be religious truth on those not disposed to accept it simply did not work — and, in any case, was wrong and constituted an injustice. The truth did not cease to be true, of course, but trying to force it upon others did not really follow from the mere fact of its being true — from the fact that the truth *was* the truth. The Catholic Church, for her part, has in no way ceased to believe that her teachings *are* true — but it has long since become equally evident that religious belief *cannot* be compelled, however compelling the truth may seem to those who believe it to be the truth.

The First Amendment to the Constitution of the United States forbidding the establishment of religion, while upholding its free exercise, was one of the solider developments on the way to seeing genuine religious freedom accepted in the way that it is pretty much accepted and respected today, especially in the Western world. However, such a fair and sensible solution to religious disagreements has hardly been a universal human phenomenon. There still remain those who believe that if something is true, it therefore ought to be compulsory. In some cases, votaries of this point of view are legion. Ironically, even some modern-day secularists — and not only the Communists! — show themselves tempted to try to impose *their* modern secularist "truths" with the same rigor or worse formerly employed in past attempts to impose religious truth. It is quite remarkable, in fact, how often we are still regularly reminded today of the violence done in the old religious wars, while the wholly secular and totalitarian ideological wars of the twentieth century — many times as coercive and bloody and destructive as the religious wars ever were — get passed over in relative silence, as if the imposition of a secularist ideology were not a problem.

As the case for religious freedom gradually developed, primarily in the Western world, the Catholic Church was relatively slow in formally agreeing as a matter of Church policy or teaching with the growing consensus that religious freedom was desirable, and, indeed, imperative. Because she was so acutely conscious of being the bearer — and the teacher and practitioner — of the fullness of Christ's revelation, that is, of being the "one true Church," the Catholic Church did not easily and automatically arrive at a definite and formulated policy on the proper theory and practice of religious freedom. After all, through her founding apostles, the Church had been *commanded* by Jesus Christ to "make disciples of all nations" (Mt 28:19), and so it was not always clear how in certain instances she might, in effect, actually have to *hold back* from always and everywhere insisting on Catholic truth as her first priority.

Of course, the Church has long since ceased to be involved in, or to acquiesce in, efforts to impose her creed on anyone, just as other Christians have mostly done the same. The very idea of imposing the creed had become almost unthinkable. Yet it was still not entirely clear on what *basis* the Church might be able or might be obliged to hold back from insisting on Catholic truth as the first priority — from continuing to insist, in other words, that her creed necessarily had to be obligatory because it was *true*!

How the Church finally arrived instead at the advocacy of religious freedom as articulated by Pope Benedict XVI in his 2009 "State of the World" address and in other statements of his and of his recent predecessors, was largely the work of the Second Vatican Council of 1962-65. As most people are aware, Vatican II made many changes in the Church's policies and practices (while reaffirming many of her essential truths). Religious liberty was only one of the areas where the Council debated and decided an issue which had previously not been completely thought through or thought out as far as the official position of the Church was concerned.

It is now more than fifty years since, on January 29, 1959, Blessed Pope John XXIII surprised the world by announcing that he intended to summon an ecumenical council of the Catholic Church. It was to be held at the Vatican in Rome, bringing together the Catholic bishops of the world to deliberate and decide about questions facing the Church in a world that had drastically changed since the previous Church council more than a century earlier. Vatican II would be the twenty-first in the long list of ecumenical councils convened by the Church in the course of her centuries-long history.

Vatican II got underway in the fall of 1962. Four sessions, each one of several months in length, were held each fall in the *aula* of St. Peter's Vatican Basilica in Rome. The Catholic bishops of the world, then numbering some 2500, thus had to travel to Rome each fall to participate in the Council. Today there are more than 4000 Catholic bishops around the world, and so if there were to be another ecumenical council, it is not clear where they could all meet together, since in the 1960s they already filled virtually to overflowing what was then the largest church in the world. The press and media of the day took a great interest in the Second Vatican Council and its proceedings were widely — and sometimes even sensationally — reported to the world at large.

Blessed Pope John XXIII died in 1963, after presiding over only the first session of Vatican II. This jovial pope had been much loved and admired. Dramatically summoning the Council in the way that he did was only one of the ways in which he seemed to present a new image of the papacy to the world. He was perhaps the first pope who was even something of a star in the new "celebrity" kind of culture created by the media, and his doings and his sometimes witty sayings were widely reported, creating a benevolent and even indulgent image of the papacy. This image was somewhat misleading, however, since Pope John XXIII insisted more strongly than anything on the truth of Catholic *teaching*, was undeviatingly orthodox in his doctrine, and was very traditional devotionally. He was no broad-minded modern "liberal" in any sense of the word.

Pope John XXIII stated in his opening address to the Council, in fact, that his principal reason for calling it was so that "the sacred deposit of Christian *doctrine* should be guarded and taught more efficaciously." That's *doctrine*, Catholic teaching, to which so many people today seem to think we ought to be allergic!

Pope John XXIII was succeeded in the chair of Peter by the archbishop of Milan, Cardinal Giovanni Battista Montini, a notable Church figure who had been a key aide to Pope Pius XII, who had occupied the chair of Peter between 1939 and 1958. Montini, although he was a very able and sophisticated prelate, was a much less effusive personality than Pope John. He took the name of Paul VI; and in his inaugural address at the second session of the Council in the fall of 1963, he included a strong call for religious freedom among other things. Paul VI presided over the final three sessions of Vatican II, and promulgated all of the Council's documents.

The Council issued sixteen documents in all, including four major constitutions. These were: the Constitution on the Sacred Liturgy, *Sacrosanctum Concilium*; the great Dogmatic Constitution on the Church, *Lumen Gentium*; the Dogmatic Constitution on Divine Revelation, *Dei Verbum*; and the Pastoral Constitution on the Church in the Modern World, *Gaudium et Spes*. The wide range and scope of the Council's work can be gauged from these four constitutions alone.

But this conciliar work ranged even more widely in the nine decrees issued by the Council: the Decree on the Means of Social Communication ("the media"), *Inter Mirifica*; the Decree on the Catholic Eastern Churches, *Orientalium Ecclesiarum*; the Decree on Ecumenism, *Unitatis Redintegratio*; the Decree on the Pastoral Office of Bishops in the Church, *Christus Dominus*; the Decree on the Up-to-date Renewal of the Religious Life, *Perfectae Caritatis*; the Decree on the Training of Priests, *Optatam Totius*; the Decree on the Ministry and Life of Priests, *Presbyterorum Ordinis*; the Decree on the Apostolate of Lay People, *Apostolicam Actuositatem*; and, finally, the Decree on the Church's Missionary Activity, *Ad Gentes Divinitus*. It should be evident from the titles of these decrees alone that the Second Vatican Council aimed at the renewal of almost every aspect of the Church's life. The Church has relied regularly and heavily on all these documents in the more than fifty years since the Council, and it is likely that she will continue to rely on them in the years to come.

Nor is that all the Council did. There remained the Council's three very important declarations, which have also governed Church policy and practice since the Council: the Declaration on Christian Education, *Gravissimum Educationis*; the Declaration on the Relation of the Church to Non-Christian Religions, *Nostra Aetate*; and the epochal Declaration on Religious Freedom, *Dignitatis Humanae*. It is this last document with which we are concerned in this book.

To summarize briefly what will be explained more fully in subsequent chapters, this Declaration on Religious Freedom, whose very title in Latin meant "human dignity," represented a major change of emphasis in the Church's teaching on the subject of religious freedom. Prior to Vatican II, Church teaching had emphasized the duty of both individuals and society itself and even the State to serve God and the (true) Catholic religion. In this perspective, a favored principle was that "error has no rights." Hence it was not seen as necessary to accord "liberty" to religious beliefs, opinions, and viewpoints that were not in accord with Catholic truth and that hence by definition were *not* true. Toleration of them seemed to be the most that could be required, and there was sometimes even some question about that.

For since the truth revealed by Christ and handed down in the Church manifestly *was* true, as the Church firmly held (and holds), all men as well as society itself and the State surely *ought* to recognize and pay homage to that truth. This was considered to be self-evident, for it was God's truth, after all, that was in question, and the same position was thus quite regularly reflected in the teachings of the popes, including such nineteenth-century popes as Blessed Pope Pius IX and Pope Leo XIII. It was similarly reflected in concordats or treaties which the Church in those days often concluded with some governments, usually in Catholic countries, which accorded special recognition and rights and privileges to the Catholic Church. The Church relies much less on such concordats today.

However, there always existed another strand in Catholic teaching that was to be found especially in the writings of such popes as Leo XIII, Pius XI, Pius XII, and John XXIII. This strand recognized and affirmed "the inviolable rights of the human person," including the right to freedom of conscience. It was this strand that Vatican II elected to emphasize and pursue when drafting and debating the Declaration on Religious Freedom, *Dig-*

nitatis Humanae, leaving intact, as the document itself expressly notes, "traditional Catholic doctrine on the moral duty of men and societies toward the true religion and toward the one Church of Christ" (DH 1).

Among the reasons for what amounted to a significant change in emphasis in the Church's teaching — a change which would lead to a more explicit affirmation of religious liberty — was the Church's experience of persecution under twentieth-century Communist, Fascist, and Nazi totalitarianisms. The rights of believers to worship God according to their consciences had to be affirmed against these and similar tyrannies. Also, the idea of a "Catholic State" continuing to be engaged in denying any standing to perceived errors contrary to Catholic teaching, increasingly represented a role which few or no modern States were any longer prepared to assume.

Thus, Vatican II consciously decided to adopt a different approach to religious liberty, one based on affirming the human dignity of the religious believer. This new emphasis was reflected in the title of *Dignitatis Humanae* itself, which *means* "on human dignity." In the document, the Catholic Church, speaking through the Council, teaches that "the human person has a *right* to religious freedom." What is entailed by this right is "that all men are to be *immune from coercion* on the part of individuals or of social groups and of every human power in such wise that no one is to be forced to act in a manner contrary to his own beliefs, whether *privately or publicly, within due limits....*"

This fundamental right to be free from coercion in religious matters is based, in the Council's thinking, on "the very *dignity of the human person* as this dignity is known through the revealed word of God and by reason itself." Moreover, this "right of the human person to religious freedom is to be recognized in the constitutional law whereby society is governed and thus it is to become a *civil right....*" Indeed, "the exercise of this right is not to be impeded provided that *just public order* be observed" — this last quoted passage explaining the "due limits" mentioned above.

Such, then, is the essence of the teaching of the Catholic Church on religious liberty, as set forth in *Dignitatis Humanae* (DH 2; emphasis added throughout). The rest of the document is mostly concerned with explaining and laying out some of the implications of this basic teaching. We shall enter more fully into what it all means as we go along, but it should be emphasized at the outset that the teaching does represent a new emphasis in what the Church has traditionally held and taught.

Biblical Abbreviations

OLD TESTAMENT

Genesis	Gn	Nehemiah	Ne	Baruch	Ba
Exodus	Ex	Tobit	Tb	Ezekiel	Ezk
Leviticus	Lv	Judith	Jdt	Daniel	Dn
Numbers	Nb	Esther	Est	Hosea	Ho
Deuteronomy	Dt	1 Maccabees	1 M	Joel	Jl
Joshua	Jos	2 Maccabees	2 M	Amos	Am
Judges	Jg	Job	Jb	Obadiah	Ob
Ruth	Rt	Psalms	Ps	Jonah	Jon
1 Samuel	1 S	Proverbs	Pr	Micah	Mi
2 Samuel	2 S	Ecclesiastes	Ec	Nahum	Na
1 Kings	1 K	Song of Songs	Sg	Habakkuk	Hab
2 Kings	2 K	Wisdom	Ws	Zephaniah	Zp
1 Chronicles	1 Ch	Sirach	Si	Haggai	Hg
2 Chronicles	2 Ch	Isaiah	Is	Malachi	Ml
Ezra	Ezr	Jeremiah	Jr	Zechariah	Zc
		Lamentations	Lm		

NEW TESTAMENT

Matthew	Mt	Ephesians	Eph	Hebrews	Heb
Mark	Mk	Philippians	Ph	James	Jm
Luke	Lk	Colossians	Col	1 Peter	1 P
John	Jn	1 Thessalonians	1 Th	2 Peter	2 P
Acts	Ac	2 Thessalonians	2 Th	1 John	1 Jn
Romans	Rm	1 Timothy	1 Tm	2 John	2 Jn
1 Corinthians	1 Cor	2 Timothy	2 Tm	3 John	3 Jn
2 Corinthians	2 Cor	Titus	Tt	Jude	Jude
Galatians	Gal	Philemon	Phm	Revelation	Rv

AFFIRMING RELIGIOUS FREEDOM

CHAPTER ONE

THE NATURE OF AND THE NEED FOR THE CHURCH'S NEW EMPHASIS ON RELIGIOUS FREEDOM

ALTHOUGH VATICAN COUNCIL II's teaching on religious freedom certainly represented a new emphasis in Church teaching, it was *not* a "new teaching" superseding an "old teaching." Blessed Pope John XXIII, in his 1963 encyclical, *Pacem in Terris*, had already anticipated the Council's teaching when he wrote that "among man's rights is that of being able to worship God in accordance with the right dictates of his own conscience, and to profess his religion both in private and in public" (PT 14). In the same way, Pope Pius XII, in an Address to Italian Jurists on December 6, 1953, had declared that "the duty of repressing religious and moral error cannot... be an ultimate norm of action. It must be subordinated to higher and more general norms which in some circumstances permit, and even perhaps make it appear the better course of action, that error should *not* be impeded to promote a greater good" (emphasis added).

Similarly, just prior to the Council itself, an Australian Catholic priest and scholar, Eric D'Arcy, who later became archbishop of Hobart, Tasmania, in Australia, correctly gauged which way the doctrinal winds were blowing when he published an excellent 1961 book on the subject entitled *Conscience and Its Right to Freedom*.

In this book, he laid out the case for religious freedom using entirely traditional Catholic sources from St. Jerome to St. Thomas Aquinas. Those who have questioned whether *Dignitatis Humanae* is in accord with traditional Catholic doctrine should look up this book written around the same time as the Council was deliberating; it reaches the same destination as Vatican II, though by a slightly different route, but the destination itself appears to be the correct one as far as Catholic teaching is concerned.

And as we shall be able to see in more detail later, the route that Vatican II took also resulted in a solid affirmation of the need for religious freedom. What this affirmation entailed was that, out of respect for the human dignity of those who did not acknowledge the truth of the Catholic faith, the Church is prepared and obliged to respect and defend their freedom to believe and practice their religion according to the dictates of their consciences, even if, objectively, they remain in error. But it was not at all as if error itself had suddenly acquired "rights"; it was that human beings possessing human dignity had rights — even the right to be wrong.

Moreover, this conciliar affirmation did not mean that the Catholic Church ceased to be the one, true Church, teaching the fullness of Christ's truth, as well as possessing the fullness of the sacramental means to sanctification and salvation for all that had originally been committed by Christ to the apostles to be handed down in the Church. On the contrary, as we shall see, *Dignitatis Humanae* specifically reaffirmed that the Catholic Church is the teacher of truth. The creed remained as true as ever, just as the sacraments were as valid as ever. What was changed was the notion that *because* Catholic religious belief was true, everyone therefore was necessarily and always obliged to accept and profess it or be subject to various sanctions and penalties wherever the Church might have the power or influence to impose or approve them. We must honestly remind ourselves that this kind of approach to religious truth *was* the sincere belief of many Christians in the past (not just Catholics, of course) — as it appears today still to be the belief of jihadists and some other religious militants in our contemporary world.

Vatican Council II, however, speaking authoritatively for the Catholic Church, decided that avoidance of the harm and injury that can result from compulsion or coercion in matters of religious belief — even if a given religious belief *is* true! — outweighs the solemn responsibility that Christians have to propagate and spread their faith. Christians *still* have that solemn responsibility, of course, but there remains also the fact that they must always go about fulfilling it in a peaceful Christian manner. There is, furthermore, and not incidentally, another important and interesting fact to be added here and that is that Vatican II's decision to affirm religious freedom was to quite a significant degree influenced by the American bishops at the Council. The way in which the Church had flourished under the American constitutional system provided both a model and an inspiration to the Council Fathers in plowing this relatively new ground, a model and inspiration that had not existed, for example, during the Council of Trent.

In this and the following short chapters, an effort will be made to explain in more detail how and why the Second Vatican Council decided to take up and deal with this very contemporary problem of religious freedom; and also to explain why significant numbers of the Council Fathers who were initially opposed to this effort were persuaded to accept it; and, finally, a similar effort will be made to clarify the nature and scope and meaning of what it was that the Council finally did decide and decree. Then, in an Appendix, the text of the Council's Declaration on Religious Freedom, *Dignitatis Humanae*, is itself included in full. It is not a long document, nor is it a complicated one, and it deserves to be read and studied in its own right.

Certainly also the Catholic Church's teaching on religious freedom ought to be better known and understood, considering that in today's world we are still regularly confronted with so many *violations* of religious freedom. Nor are these violations confined only to the terrorist acts which today's jihadists believe to be in the service of their religious truth. Among the first acts of the new government of Iraq, for example, which came to power as a result of the war *against* terrorism, have been measures which are now causing Iraqi Christians to leave that country in increasing numbers. Recent press reports speak of a "mass exodus of Christians from the Middle East and the lack of full religious freedom there" (CNS report, 2/9/09). Some of these Christian communities have lived in the region for centuries — since antiquity — but today they are being driven into exile because their freedom to worship in accordance with Christina truth is not respected.

Nor is this a phenomenon confined to historically Muslim countries. A recent paper by the Hudson Institute, for example, records that:

> On August 23, 2008, violence reignited against the Christians of Orissa state in India when an extremist Hindu leader was killed by suspected Maoist rebels. Though Maoists took responsibility for the killing, the Hindu leaders embarked on a large-scale campaign of arson and killing against the Christian community. According to news reports, by October 13, over 60 Christians had been killed and 18,000 wounded; 181 churches razed or destroyed; 4,500 Christian homes burned and more than 50,000 Christians were displaced, of whom more than 30,000 remain in refugee camps or in hiding in the jungle. The local government failed to take effective measures to quell the violence, and the central government was slow in responding to this crisis.
>
> The religious violence in Orissa was enflamed by accusations from hard line Hindu organizations and

their political parties that Christian churches have been "forcibly" converting the local population. Although India's Constitution guarantees religious freedom to all of its citizens, Hindu political parties demand laws to curb the conversion of Hindus to other faiths.

Pope Benedict XVI was certainly on track, then, when he spoke about the plight of Christian communities in Asia in his 2009 "State of the World" address. As the Hudson Institute paper just quoted notes, India is a country with a constitution that is supposed to guarantee religious freedom both to individuals and communities, just as *Dignitatis Humanae* specifies. That this constitutional guarantee could nevertheless be so easily set aside, as in this case, surely underlines the seriousness of the contemporary problem of religious freedom — or the lack of it! — in the world today. And, of course, other examples could be cited, for example, China.

Indeed, modern secular governments in general can be cited for failure to respect religious freedom in important ways, for instance, in some of the countries in the European Union. Similarly, if we are paying any attention to the rhetoric of the diehard votaries of the separation of Church and State in the United States, we will realize that potential threats to the freedom of religion guaranteed by the First Amendment to the Constitution exist here as well. Respected commentators have noted that, even while the First Amendment's prohibition of the "establishment" of any religion by Congress is sometimes carried to absurd lengths in judicial decisions and in other ways, the same First Amendment's guarantee of the "free exercise" of religion is less often practiced or cited.

Many readers will thus want to pursue the concrete problem of religious freedom in the world today. Some might wish to begin with the recent book of Thomas F. Farr published by the Oxford University Press in 2008 entitled: *World of Faith and Freedom: Why International Religious Freedom Is Vital to American Na-*

tional Security. This book provides interesting and persuasive perspectives on the whole problem, as well as identifying sources for further reading.

It must be emphasized, however, that the present book is *not* about the problems of religious freedom that exist *today*. The present book is about how, some fifty years ago, at Vatican Council II, the Catholic Church developed her traditional teaching on human dignity in a way that resulted in a cogent *reasoned theory* of why there ought to be religious freedom, a theory that affirms religious freedom *in principle* (and not just as something to be tolerated, perhaps grudgingly). Many secularist or secularizing thinkers today believe that religious freedom is only possible if religious truth claims are laid aside and religion is merely tolerated as essentially a matter of private and personal belief. This is the dominant view of religious freedom among secularists in America today, in fact.

The Church's teaching, however, sees things differently. It provides a *basis*, human dignity, on which to affirm that both individuals and communities *ought* to be free to practice their religion, according to their consciences, both in public and in private — at the same time that the Church should be free to "proclaim upon the housetops" (Mt 10:27) the truths of Christ's Gospel. Christ's Gospel is *not*, and cannot be, merely a matter of private and personal belief!

Precisely in view of the parlous state of religious freedom in the world today, though, it is to be hoped that both the teaching and the example of the Catholic Church will contribute to a better understanding of what religious freedom is and ought to be — and perhaps will also contribute even to the development of an international consensus on both the desirability and, indeed, the necessity, of religious freedom. Such a development would indisputably make for a better world and is eminently worth working for! Whatever the future may hold in this regard, however, the Catholic

Church can certainly be confident that her venture into the whole area of religious freedom at Vatican Council II truly resulted in the enunciation of truths that the world needs to know about and, especially, to heed. The Council Fathers at Vatican II truly decided better than they perhaps knew.

CHAPTER TWO

WHAT THE SECOND VATICAN COUNCIL
ACTUALLY DECIDED AND WHY

V ATICAN COUNCIL II's Declaration on Religious Freedom, *Dignitatis Humanae* ("Of Human Dignity"), approved and promulgated only the day before the Council itself ended on December 8, 1965, was one of the shortest of all the sixteen documents issued by the Council. Along with the Council's three great Constitutions, however, it was certainly one of the most important documents that the Council produced. Pope Paul VI would later call it one of the Council's "major texts" and "greatest documents." It is the only Vatican II document in which it is expressly stated that the Council Fathers intended to *develop* what they called "the doctrine of recent popes on the inviolable rights of the human person" (DH 1). It was also one of the most debated and controversial of the Vatican II documents, both during and after the Council. It remains fundamental today, as it also remains quite controversial in some circles.

The conciliar *schema*, or draft text, known as the Religious Liberty Declaration, began as a chapter of what became the Council's Decree on Ecumenism, *Unitatis Redintegratio*, and only achieved independent status later in its third version. It has been pointed out that three of the Council's most important documents, *Unitatis Redintegratio* on ecumenism, *Nostra Aetate* on relations with non-Christians (and, significantly, with the Jews), and *Dignitatis Humanae* itself on religious freedom, were all basically the products of German Cardinal Augustin Bea's Secretariat for Promoting Christian Unity (SPCU).

Cardinal Bea, a Jesuit priest and a distinguished biblical scholar in his day, was one of the favorites of the pope who convoked the Second Vatican Council, Blessed John XXIII. Pope John encouraged the work of Cardinal Bea's Secretariat for Promoting Christian Unity to an unusual degree. It was not one of the regular congregations of the Roman Curia; nor was it one of the conciliar commissions created and assigned to prepare the work of the Council. Normally it would not have counted for much in the way things are set up in the Roman Curia, the permanent staff organization of the Holy See. But Blessed John XXIII had great confidence in Cardinal Bea and so, contrary to the views of some of the officials in the Roman Curia, as well as of some of the bishops at the Council itself, he gave the relatively newly founded Secretariat for Christian Unity its head. As a result, it turned out to be one of the more important and productive entities within the conciliar structure. Eventually it did become a permanent entity within the Roman Curia under the name of the Pontifical Council for Promoting Christian Unity (PCPCU), and it continues to function under that name today.

The chapter of the original ecumenism *schema* which eventually became the religious liberty *schema* started out as a treatment of the Church and State issue generally, but this was quickly seen as much too broad a topic for the Council to attempt to cover, and so it was cut back to the issue of religious freedom alone. It went through some six different versions in all. Three formal debates on the *schema* took place in the *aula* of St. Peter's in the course of which some 120 speeches were delivered by individual bishops. In addition, more than 600 written interventions were sent to the Secretariat for Promoting Christian Unity concerning the *schema*.

More than 2000 separate *modi*, or suggested amendments, were considered before the final text was approved. The issue of religious freedom was manifestly one of the most controversial and most thoroughly debated of all the issues at the Council.

Thus, *Dignitatis Humanae* was definitely considered by many what we call a "hot potato," and the debates about it were both spirited and sustained. Its importance was fully recognized at the time however the final text was eventually going to read. It might be asked: what made it so important? The short answer is that, for the first time in her long history, the Catholic Church formally and explicitly declared as an official teaching of hers that "the human person has a *right* to religious freedom" (DH 2; emphasis added).

A right. To religious freedom. But what does the Church mean by the "religious freedom," to which the Council was declaring that the human person had a "right"? The Declaration itself specifies that "this freedom means that all men are to be *immune from coercion* on the part of individuals or of social groups and of any human power in such wise that no one is to be forced to act in a manner contrary to his own beliefs, whether privately or publicly, whether alone or in association with others, within due limits." The only qualification of or limitation on the exercise of this right thus recognized by the Council is that "just public order be observed," that is, not violated (DH 2 & 3; emphasis added).

What is the basis of this right to religious freedom affirmed by the Council? It "has its foundation," the Declaration specifies, "in the very *dignity of the human person* as this dignity is known through the revealed Word of God and by reason itself." Moreover, "this right of the human person to religious freedom is to be recognized in the constitutional law whereby society is governed and thus it is to become a *civil right*" (DH 2; emphasis added). The emphasis on the civil character of the right is important; the Council Fathers were primarily concerned with the issue as it was typically manifested in civil society (and not, for instance, in the Church). The Declaration was actually given a descriptive subtitle by the Council, as follows: "On the Right of the Person and of Communities to Social and Civil Freedom in Matters Religious." It is noteworthy that civil freedom is what is specified. The Council Fathers were addressing a problem *in* civil society.

It is noteworthy that the Council was also concerned here with the question of *human dignity*. This was the case not only in the document *Dignitatis Humanae* itself, but in a number of the other conciliar documents as well. The subject of human dignity was one of the major themes of the Second Vatican Council, as a matter of fact. For example, the Council's Pastoral Constitution on the Church in the Modern World, *Gaudium et Spes*, devotes an entire lengthy chapter to the same subject (GS 12-22). This latter document grounds human dignity in the fact that man was created in the image of God — "male and female he created them" (Gn 1:27) — and it specifically states that "the dignity of man rests above all on the fact that he is called to communion with God" (GS 19). *Gaudium et Spes* returns more than once to the same subject beyond the confines of the specific chapter devoted to it. In dealing with the "common good," for example, it speaks of "the sublime dignity of the human person" (GS 26); and, in a passage which was a particular favorite of Pope John Paul II quoted many times by him, *Gaudium et Spes* stresses the uniqueness of the dignity of "the only creature on earth that God wanted for its own sake" (GS 24).

Still other conciliar documents stress the same thing. The Declaration on the Relation of the Church to Non-Christian Religions, *Nostra Aetate*, in which, among other things, the Church affirms her respect for the Jewish people and rejects anti-Semitism in any form, goes on to reject discrimination of any kind against any people "on the basis of their race, color, condition in life, or religion." In plain words, *Nostra Aetate* states that "there is no basis... either in theory or in practice for any discrimination between individual and individual, or between people and people, arising either from *human dignity* or from the rights which flow from it" (NA; emphasis added). As the Council saw it, human dignity was the basis upon which discrimination was to be rejected, just as it was the basis upon which religious liberty was to be affirmed.

Similarly, the Council's Decree on Education, *Gravissimum Educationis*, declares that "all men of whatever race, condition, or age, in virtue of their *dignity as human persons*, have an inalienable right to education" (GE 1; emphasis again added).

Thus, the subject of human dignity is foundational in a number of the Council's documents besides the eponymous religious freedom Declaration itself under examination here. It should not, however, be thought that this affirmation of the importance of human dignity was in any sense a new Church teaching. On the contrary, the importance of human dignity has often been affirmed in Church teaching. For example, in his famous 1891 encyclical *Rerum Novarum*, Pope Leo XIII wrote that "no one may with impunity outrage the dignity of man, which God himself treats with great reverence" (RN 57).

So while taking up again the subject of human dignity, the Council was not venturing into completely unknown territory; nor was it enunciating or expatiating on any uniquely *revealed* Catholic doctrine or dogma. Rather, it was essentially — in some ways rather tardily, in fact — aligning the Church behind principles already widely accepted in modern democratic societies and enshrined, for example, in such documents as the 1789 Constitution of the United States and the 1948 United Nations Universal Declaration on Human Rights.

One very important thing about the whole conciliar process of debating and approving *Dignitatis Humanae* was that, owing to the particular history of the Church in Europe (where "established Churches" had been the norm for many centuries, and in traditionally Catholic countries the focus had long been on the obligations of the State towards the true religion), the question of the basic right of the human person to be free from coercion in religious matters had never been adequately focused on and articulated in Catholic teaching. Owing to the great interest in the subject in modern democratic states, however, the Church was already moving, well before the Council, towards a clearer expression of her own mind on the question. As we have already noted, in his last encyclical *Pacem in Terris* ("Peace on Earth") which Blessed Pope John XXIII issued on April 11, 1963, the saintly pontiff, basing his words on those of his predecessors, Leo XIII, Pius XI, and Pius XII, was already affirming "the right (of the individual) to worship according to the right dictates of his own conscience and to profess his religion both in private and in public" (PT 14).

Nevertheless, it remains true that Vatican II's Declaration on Religious Freedom finally addressed the question squarely and provided the Church with a definitive answer to it. The whole process, as well as the Declaration which resulted from it, proved to be especially controversial, though, because many Catholics believed that any such forthright assertion of a general human right to religious liberty would contradict the Church's traditional firm and repeated teachings concerning the moral obligation of all without exception to seek the truth revealed by God and to embrace it willingly in God's Church. To allow religious error to be placed on the same level as religious truth — as the question was commonly formulated — was believed to amount to granting that, contrary to the received view in the Church, error somehow *did* have rights; and, furthermore, this was thought to lead to religious indifferentism, many times condemned by the Church's magisterium.

In the context of the system of European State Churches that developed in Europe following the Protestant Reformation and the wars of religion in the sixteenth and seventeenth centuries, the moral obligation of all to seek the truth and embrace it in the

Catholic Church was based on the principle that "error has no rights." For example, in his Address to Italian Jurists of December 6, 1953, which we have already quoted, Pope Pius XII declared that "that which does not correspond to the truth and to the moral norm has objectively no right either of existence or of self-propagation or of action." This way of formulating the question — and, as stated, is certainly true enough — was usually taken to mean that only Catholics and the Catholic Church, being in full possession of the truths of God, also had a right to full religious freedom in the true sense of the word. All other Christians and Christian confessions, being under the sway of error in one degree or another, were therefore thought to be entitled only to *tolerance*; and perhaps also to a measure of understanding dictated by prudential judgment; but certainly not to any "right" to profess religious error. This was long the common view, even though Pope Pius XII, as we have already noted, went on to note that *not* to impede error by means of laws and coercive measures can nevertheless be justified in the interest of a superior and more extensive good. Hence the notion that "error has no rights," although it held sway for a long time, was never considered an absolute principle.

Still, the State was seen as generally obligated to support the true religion, although it was recognized in practice that this could only be realized in countries with a majority of Catholics. The prevailing theory for a long time, in fact, was that this was the "ideal" State, and for this among other reasons the Church vigorously opposed the progressive secularization of society and of the State. Yet if and when the Church was disestablished, or in situations where Catholics were in a minority, the Church still claimed the freedom to operate and carry out her God-given functions to preach and sanctify. This meant in practice that Catholics were always supposed to be granted religious freedom to worship in accordance with the tenets of their faith; but if Catholics were in the majority, the same right was *not* supposed to be accorded to non-Catholics in equal measure by the "ideal" Catholic State (because the non-Catholics, by definition, were not worshipping in accordance with the true religion).

Although this theory of Church-State relations was understandable because of the way it developed historically in what had once been "Catholic Europe," it was really not completely consistent and, baldly stated — that Catholics had a right to religious freedom, but others not — it hardly did great credit to the Church. Yet it more or less persisted as the dominant theory in the Church up until the time of Vatican II, and it was considered to be the firm and fixed position of the Church by not a few, including many bishops and officials of the Holy See.

During the Council, a determined minority of bishops grounded in this way of thinking strongly opposed the *schema* on religious liberty that became *Dignitatis Humanae* primarily on the old traditional grounds that "error has no rights." A larger number had serious doubts and misgivings about whether a general right to religious liberty could be adequately formulated and stated without undermining or even contradicting the traditional Church teachings concerning the one true Church and the obligations of both individuals and States towards that Church. Many bishops found it hard to recognize that, while error manifestly does not have any "rights," human persons, even those in error, do have rights.

French Archbishop Marcel Lefebvre (who, following the Council was to be the leader of the schismatic-type movement that came to bear his name, in part because of his doubts concerning *Digntatis Humanae*), early on referred to the religious liberty *schema* as "an inconceivable *schema*." During the final debate on it in September, 1965, the French archbishop stated the basic traditionalist objection to the idea of religious liberty probably as well as anyone else ever did:

> The *schema* recognizes equal rights for all religions and
> recommends the neutrality of the State, which would

intervene only for reasons of the common good. The reporter said that this conception was arrived at after a long evolution. But it only goes back to the eighteenth century; it cannot therefore be considered traditional. The real sources of this *schema* are the philosophers of the eighteenth century — Hobbes, Hume, Locke, Rousseau, and the liberal Catholicism of Félicité de Lamennais, which was condemned by [the pope]. Should the conservation of public order be the norm for intervention on the part of the State? Communists do not hesitate to persecute Catholics in the name of this principle. Should human dignity be the basis of religious liberty? But the Communists attack our religion, which they consider an alienation, in the name of this principle.

Non-Catholic approval of this *schema* is indicative. A Freemason has written that he puts all his hope in a positive vote. Protestants also want this. In reality, this *schema* is based neither on tradition nor on Scripture, but on a false Rousseauistic conception....

The Catholic Church alone has a strict right to liberty. With regard to other communities and religions, each particular case must be examined.

Archbishop Lefebvre saw religious liberty as equivalent to the veritable license into which the French Revolution had transformed the word "liberty," just as he saw Vatican II's emphasis on ecumenism as equivalent to the French Revolution's version of "fraternity" ("Fraternity with Communists!" he fumed). Similarly, the French archbishop saw the episcopal collegiality which was also so greatly stressed at Vatican II as stemming from the dubious "equality," as he saw it, promoted by the same French Revolution. The post-Vatican II Lefebvrist movement was thus based primarily on doubts concerning the doctrinal teachings of Vatican II, and not merely, or even primarily, on disagreements concerning the reformed liturgy or the New Order of the Mass.

The great majority of the bishops at Vatican II, however, favored the *schema* on religious liberty and were also determined that the Council should go on record on the subject. This was especially true of the Eastern European bishops then living under Communism, where religious freedom was expressly denied to individuals and groups by the power of the State. The young archbishop of Cracow, Karol Wojtyla, for example, strongly supported the *schema* in an intervention delivered on September 26, 1964. As he would do so often during his pontificate later, the future Pope John Paul II stressed the idea of the dignity of the human person on which the religious liberty *schema* itself was based. "The human person, contrary to what materialistic and atheistic philosophy holds, is not an economic pawn, but is transcendental," Archbishop Wojtyla insisted. His principal reservation was that the *schema* did not emphasize strongly enough the dictum of Christ that it is the truth that will make us free (cf. Jn 8:32).

Other bishops living under Communism were equally eloquent in favor of the *schema*. During the debate on a revised text a year later, on September 21, 1965, the archbishop of Prague, Josef Beran, making his first appearance at the Council after many years in a Communist prison, was greeted with a sustained ovation when he arose to speak. He urged that "the Declaration should be addressed to governments; they should be requested to stop interfering with religious liberty, to release imprisoned priests and laymen, to permit bishops and priests to resume their functions, to leave the Church free to govern herself, to let religious congregations revive, and to give real freedom to Christian families."

As these Eastern European bishops saw things, the basic problem was no longer one of trying to get governments in Catholic countries to recognize and uphold and defend the faith by means

of the law and action of the State, but rather to get secular governments of all types to uphold any basic human rights at all. The very
idea of an established Church or a Catholic "confessional" State
seemed more and more unrelated to the reality of what the world
had become. Yet theory had not kept pace with reality, and in
the United States, for example, up to the time of the Council, the
theory remained dominant that if Catholics were ever to become
a majority, they would be obliged to seek the "establishment" of
the Church in spite of the constitutional separation of Church and
State that obtained here. Of course, it was not likely that Catholics
would be in the majority any time soon, and so the question was
not regarded as very important. Nevertheless, the principled basis
for the Church's position still remained pretty uncertain — which
did not prevent many bishops at the Council from holding to it
anyway, sometimes almost reflexively.

In the course of the very lively conciliar debates on the
religious liberty *schema*, many of those who opposed it seemed
generally to stand pat with what they understood the Church's
traditional position to be, and this pretty much because it *was* the
Church's traditional position. They were not looking at the new and
changed world out there — which perhaps required a different and
more realistic response from the Church.

Thus, for example, Cardinal José Bueno y Monreal, archbishop of Seville, Spain, opined that, "doctrinally speaking, only
one religion has the right of propagation. The others have not.
But it is a different question on the political level. Any liberty that
harms others must be restricted, the *schema* says. But liberty for
false religions harms the true religion." Auxiliary Spanish Bishop
Anastasio Granados Garcia of Toledo thought that "the doctrine
expounded here is contrary to Catholic tradition, according to
which only truth has rights. Is this progress? No. It is impossible to
put truth and error on the same plane." Another Spanish bishop,
José Lopez Ortiz, alleged that the *schema* "gives the impression

of attacking the Catholic State. There are still, happily, Catholic States. It is too bad there aren't more of them." These Spanish bishops were surely incapable of imagining the day — which has in fact now come about today — when formerly "Catholic Spain," under a leftist, Socialist government, would be promoting divorce, abortion, so-called "same-sex marriage," and other evils and follies typical of the modern secular State. But the attitudes of the Spanish bishops at Vatican II were not untypical of their times; many Catholics took for granted then what these bishops expressed.

Again, Brazilian Bishop Antonio de Castro Mayer, who, along with French Archbishop Marcel Lefebvre, would move into an actual separatist or schismatic-type situation after the Council, declared that "the doctrine exposed here is altogether opposed to the traditional doctrine of Leo XIII and Pius XII, which holds that error has no rights but that it may be granted rights to avoid a greater evil. It is absurd to say that someone in error is worthy of honor." Others who opposed the *schema* mostly did not venture far from this line of argumentation.

And as should have been expected, the more conservative leaders at the Council such as the Irish Dominican Cardinal Michael Browne, the Italian Curia Cardinal Alfredo Ottaviani, head of the Holy Office (later the Congregation for the Doctrine of the Faith), and the Archbishop of Palermo, Cardinal Ernesto Ruffini, all rose to argue forcefully against the *schema*. Cardinal Browne thought it was incorrect to give equal status to a conscience that adheres to the truth and to one that adheres to falsehood, even though sincere; and he also considered it a violation of public morality to allow the propagation of other faiths in Catholic countries. Cardinal Ottaviani affirmed that "the principle that each individual has the right to follow his own conscience must suppose that conscience is not contrary to the divine law," and he believed that the right to religious freedom "objectively belongs to those who are the members of the true religion." In the years immediately preceding the

Council, Cardinal Ottaviani had expressly and publicly defended the position that only adherents of the true (Catholic) faith possessed religious freedom in the true sense. Cardinal Ruffini pointed out that there was only one true religion, and while tolerance must be practiced, care should be taken by the Council not to appear to endorse religious indifferentism; he also objected to the suggestion in the text of the draft *schema* that the state was not entitled to grant special favors to any one religion.

The Council Fathers who favored the *schema*, however, such as the Archbishop of Chicago, Cardinal Albert Meyer, and the Archbishop of Vienna, Cardinal Franz König, argued with equal force (and mostly greater cogency) in favor of it. Cardinal Meyer said that the schema should be accepted because it reaffirmed the teaching of the recent popes, and clarified the traditional doctrine; he thought that by affirming the dignity of the person in this area the Church would demonstrate that true religion consisted in the free and generous subjection of the individual to the Creator. Cardinal König thought that the Church should not be silent regarding the tragic fact that nations existed where there was no religious freedom.

By the fourth session of the Council, in 1965, the Archbishop of Westminster in England, John Heenan, by then wearing a cardinal's hat himself, expressed the views of what appeared to be a growing number of bishops in favor of the proposed *schema*:

> We must put an end to the accusation that the Church claims liberty when she is a minority and suppresses it when she is in the majority. We must recall the not too distant *historical* circumstances when Catholics and Protestants persecuted each other and accepted the principle *cuius regio, eius religio....* This intolerance has disappeared....
> Yet some still hold that error has no rights. But per-

sons have rights, whether they are right or wrong, and the *schema* affirms this.

The principle that each must obey his conscience is indisputable. Cardinal Newman said he obeyed his conscience first and then the pope.

After much debate and many revisions, particularly about how the arguments should be framed, the issue was in the end going to be decided by the Council pretty much along the lines articulated here by Cardinal Heenan.

CHAPTER THREE

THE AMERICAN INPUT AND INFLUENCE AT THE COUNCIL

ONE SPECIAL AND UNIQUE feature of the conciliar debates on the religious liberty *schema* at the Second Vatican Council was the strong and practically unanimous support given to it by the bishops of the United States. By and large the American bishops at the Council were not at first very prominent or influential, nor did they operate as any kind of a bloc. Different bishops had very different views on the reform of the liturgy, for example, and on many other issues as well. But the American bishops, it turned out, were solid in their support of an affirmation by the Church of the principles of religious liberty. Many of them believed such principles were embodied in the American political and constitutional system and had contributed to the flourishing of the Church in the United States. They thought such principles *ought* to be promoted by the universal Church.

Cincinnati Archbishop Karl Alter was the first to call for a declaration by the Council on the subject of religious freedom. New York's Cardinal Francis Spellman along with more than 200 other bishops petitioned the Council in the same vein. Cardinals Richard Cushing of Boston, Albert Meyer of Chicago, Joseph Ritter of St. Louis, and Lawrence Shehan of Baltimore, among others, all rose to contribute major interventions on the floor on the subject of religious liberty, some of them more than once.

During the crucial debate on the *schema* during the third session in 1964, for example, Boston's Cardinal Richard J. Cushing gave his reasons why it was imperative to approve the religious liberty *schema* that was before the Council:

> We are dealing here with a question that is essential for the life of the Church and for civil life. This is the first time that the Church has solemnly expressed her doctrine on this point. All men are waiting to see what we will say. It is a crucial issue for America. Should we amend this text? If it be for the purpose of making it stronger, yes; to weaken it, never! It must remain intact. The Church must declare herself the protagonist of religious liberty in the world.
>
> Throughout history the Church has demanded liberty for herself. She has a right to it. Today she demands a similar liberty for all men without exception. The doctrinal principles which form the basis of this right to religious liberty are contained in the encyclical *Pacem in Terris*, which has had great repercussions everywhere.

Chicago's Cardinal Albert Meyer was no less emphatic, speaking in the same vein as his Boston colleague:

> The *schema* is very necessary, and men of our time expect this declaration. Let us demonstrate that what is essential is a free and sincere conscience. The *schema* will make ecumenical dialogue possible. We must take our stand on this platform of the rights of the human person. Without this declaration, our separated brethren would doubt our sincerity, and with good reason. Without this declaration, whatever else the Council might say would not be accepted by the world.

Indeed, in more ways than one, the Declaration on Religious Freedom could be said to have been America's most important contribution to the work of the Second Vatican Council. It was not just that the American bishops were solidly behind the idea, and made their strong support for it count at various junctures in the conciliar process. In another sense, the very idea of any conciliar statement on religious liberty at all had been inspired in a significant way by the American example. The idea had also been pioneered and promoted by an American theologian, Father John Courtney Murray, S.J., best known for his work reconciling the principles of American constitutional democracy with Catholic teaching as set forth, for example, in his well-known 1960 book *We Hold These Truths: Catholic Reflections on the American Proposition.* Father Murray had also long since developed a solid expertise on the questions of Church and State and religious freedom generally, having authored many scholarly articles on these topics.

Father Murray's work was not in good odor with Cardinal Alfredo Ottaviani's Holy Office in the pre-conciliar period, however — for a time he was actually forbidden by his religious superiors to write and publish on Church and State issues. Because of this, he was not initially invited to take part in the work of any of the conciliar Preparatory Commissions or to be a *peritus*, or theological expert, at the Council itself. Nor was he even present in Rome at all during the first session. Through the good offices of New York's Cardinal Francis J. Spellman, however, he was present from the second session on as a personal *peritus* of Cardinal Spellman's. Inevitably, he was called upon to work upon the successive drafts of what became *Dignitatis Humanae.*

Because of Father Murray's eminence, if not pre-eminence, in the field of Church-State relations and religious liberty in those days, some have perhaps even exaggerated his contribution to the finished conciliar Declaration. He was the principal writer of two of the successive drafts of it, though the final draft was drawn up by other hands after Father Murray had become sidelined with illness, and included significant material that Father Murray had not seen fit to include in the drafts he worked on. The fact is, of course — as is abundantly clear from the Council's history and records — that all of the sixteen Vatican II documents were the work of many hands, and this Declaration was no exception. But there is no denying that Father Murray had great influence both in how the document was drawn up and how it ultimately came out.

Yet, Father Murray, who died in 1967, soon after the end of the Council, was himself not entirely happy with the final product. He accepted the teaching, but he had questions about the adequacy of some of the arguments in favor of it. While there can be no doubt that he made a great contribution to it overall in helping to draft and refine the Declaration, and also in contributing a set of notes to the finished text as found in the Abbott edition of *The Documents of Vatican II*, Father Murray's interpretation of it does not constitute the last word on the subject. For it seems that, in his Church-State research, he had come to the conclusion that an affirmation of religious freedom by the Church entailed severely downplaying or even dropping what the Declaration itself would eventually call — a passage already quoted — the "traditional Catholic doctrine on the moral duty of men and societies toward the true religion and toward the one Church of Christ" (DH 1) — a formulation added to a later draft of the text than the drafts Father Murray had worked on. The Council Fathers understood, as Father Murray apparently did not, that this "traditional Catholic doctrine" was an irreformable doctrine and could not be changed or dropped, even though the Church now wished to affirm and emphasize religious liberty. Nevertheless, Father Murray's notes to the text of *Dignitatis Humanae* remain valuable in interpreting it, and we shall refer to them more than once.

All in all, the American contribution to Vatican II, which in many ways was secondary as far as the Council as a whole was concerned (especially by comparison with the work of, for instance, the European Alliance, which consisted of mostly progressive bishops from Western Europe), became much more prominent in the preparation and approval of the Declaration on Religious Freedom. Apparently, the efforts of the American bishops were crucial in getting the document approved. An anonymous American bishop is quoted in more than one of the histories of the Council as having said that without the support of the American bishops, "this document would not have reached the floor."

What happened was that the latest draft distributed towards the end of the third session was found to have been changed enough from the earlier draft so that the very conservative *Coetus Internationalis Patrum*, or International Group of Fathers, was able to argue that it was, in effect, a new document, and hence it fell under Council rules requiring an adequate period between the time the bishops were given the text, and the time when a vote could be taken on it. This meant a delay in the consideration of the document on the floor. What this required delay meant was that there would be no time left for a vote on the religious liberty *schema* during the third session in 1964. The opponents of the *schema* had failed to stop its progress in the course of the debate up to that point, but now they saw a procedural way to keep the document from coming to the floor for a vote — perhaps forever, as these opponents hoped, and as the proponents of the *schema* among the Council Fathers feared.

An indefatigable Italian bishop, Luigi Carli of Segni, Italy, who was a prominent member of the conservative *Coetus*, drew up a letter asking for a delay in the vote and citing the applicable Council rules. With all that was going on, the Council Presidency seems to have been quite happy to agree with such a request for a delay in this particular case. As soon as word about this got out, however, the American bishops, among others, were greatly alarmed, fearing that the *schema* might indeed be tabled forever, since the opposition to it had persisted and both substantive and procedural objections to it continued to be raised. The request for another delay, in fact, was only the latest in a series of maneuvers against the *schema*.

Cardinal Albert Meyer of Chicago, one of the Council Presidents, was one of the *schema's* strongest proponents, as we have already noted, and he quickly helped draw up a petition to the Holy Father himself protesting the deferral of the vote. Cardinals Joseph Ritter of St. Louis and Paul-Émile Léger of Montreal, Canada, joined Cardinal Meyer in personally going to see Pope Paul VI on the matter. Father Ralph Wiltgen, S.V.D., in his excellent history of the Council, *The Rhine Flows into the Tiber*, describes the whole scene on what proved to be one of the most tumultuous days ever at the Second Vatican Council:

> [They] decided on the wording of a special petition to be circulated immediately. It was the famous *instanter, instantius, instantissme* petition to the Holy Father consisting of only one sentence: "Reverently but insistently, more insistently, most insistently, we request that the vote on the Declaration on Religious Freedom be allowed to take place before the end of this Council session, lest the confidence of the Christian and the non-Christian world be lost." Angry bishops meanwhile poured from their stalls and formed excited groups. Copies of the petition passed rapidly from hand to hand. Never had there been such a furious signing of names, such confusion, such agitation. Never had there been such wild and harsh words as in this moment of panic, when it seemed that a cherished Council document might be tabled forever.

The signed petitions were quickly collected and given to Cardinal Meyer, who had meanwhile been joined by Cardinals Ritter and Léger. Together they left the Council hall while the meeting was still in progress and went to see the pope, begging him to overrule the decision.

It would no doubt have been most uncharacteristic of Pope Paul VI simply to overrule a firm conciliar decision. Except where doctrinal integrity was concerned, this pope almost always preferred accommodation and sought consensus. The three North American cardinals evidently did succeed in getting the pontiff's attention, however. What Paul VI agreed to, however, was that the religious liberty *schema* would be taken up as the first order of business at the fourth session of the Council in 1965.

This still did not mean, however, that the *schema* would necessarily be approved. The opposition to it continued without respite. Bishop Luigi Carli of Segni, again along with the *Coetus*, or International Group of Fathers, submitted many more amendments. In July, 1965, prior to the opening of the fourth session, Archbishop Geraldo de Proença Sigaud of Diamantina, Brazil, Archbishop Marcel Lefebvre of the Holy Ghost Fathers, and Abbott John Prou of the Benedictine Abbey of Solesmes in France wrote directly to the Holy Father concerning the changes they still wished to see in the text. Yet other groups and bishops raised questions. The tensions and pressures were terrific. It should not be forgotten, however, that all these pressures resulted in some successive additions to the text that, in the end, made it possible for the text to be approved as an authentic expression of the true mind of the Church. It was generally the conservatives who insisted that certain things had to be included *if* the document was to be approved by the Council; but as believers we may be confident that, *since* this was an ecumenical Council of the Catholic Church, after all, the workings and influence of the Holy Spirit were also not entirely absent or passive in all of these movements and proceedings.

Among other issues, the conservatives thought that the criterion limiting the exercise of religious freedom should be the *common good* and not just the preservation of the *public order*. Some of the other amendments proposed by the opposition actually seemed to make good sense, as this one seemed to, and some of them were added in to the text in various ways.

By and large, however, neither the substantive amendments nor the procedural maneuvers of the conservatives succeeded in changing the outcome by very much. The conservatives were largely given short shrift, in fact, and were even criticized by the management of the Council for exerting the kinds of pressures which the liberal European Alliance of bishops had been employing at the Council pretty much with impunity all along. To what extent this kind of dismissive treatment of at least some of the conservative concerns contributed to the state of mind that later eventuated in the Lefebvrist separatist movement cannot easily be gauged. By the fourth session, however, it had become pretty clear that both the pope and a rather large Council majority were determined to have a Declaration on Religious Freedom, regardless of the continuing opposition to it by some bishops.

Because Pope Paul VI was going to New York to address the United Nations in the fall of 1965, two months before the end of the Council, it became unmistakably clear that the pontiff himself wanted the Council to be clear on the world's public record in favor of religious liberty. The pope was even insisting on a timely preliminary vote on the *schema* to that effect in order to demonstrate which way the Council was going. We know this because after the steering committee had voted yet again to defer a vote on the measure, on the morning of September 26, 1965, the Council's President, Cardinal Eugène Tisserant, its Cardinal Moderator, Cardinal Gregory Agagianian, and its Secretary General of the Council, Archbishop Pericle Felici, all arrived late and breathless in the *aula* of St. Peter's, having come directly from the papal apartments. It was then suddenly announced that, in accordance with the wishes of "higher authority," there *would* be a preliminary vote on the religious freedom *schema*.

There was such a preliminary vote. 1997 Council Fathers voted *placet* to approve the *schema*, 224 voted *non placet* to disapprove, and there was one null ballot. It was henceforth now absolutely clear that by the end of the Council, the body would definitely be going on record in favor of religious liberty, and by a rather large majority at that. Perhaps the issue had never really been in doubt, despite all the maneuvering and the heated passions that were almost invariably aroused by the mere mention of the topic — and despite the persistence and even ingenuity of the conservative minority opposition to it. As we have noted, the conservative opposition did succeed in modifying the draft so that in the end it confined itself to rather narrowly stating the strict case for religious liberty, while leaving intact the Church's traditional teaching on the obligation of persons and societies to seek the true religion and to adhere to it.

After yet further minor revisions, the votes against the *schema* dropped down to 70, while on the day before the Council ended, December 8, 1965, no less than 2308 Council Fathers again gave the Declaration another one of the large majorities that nearly all of the conciliar documents eventually garnered. No doubt some bishops who had opposed the *schema* were reconciled to it in the end *because* it was on its way to be approved by such a large majority. The influence of the Holy Spirit did seem to be a factor in the *schema*'s favor — as did that of the American bishops, who were particularly elated at the ultimate outcome, and believed correctly that their efforts and interventions had been crucial in helping bring about the final approval of the Declaration. Chicago's Cardinal Meyer, however, never lived to see the vindication of his own major role in the whole affair. He fell ill after the end of the tumultuous third session of the Council in 1964 during which he had acted so vigorously, and he died of a brain tumor some five months before the beginning of the fourth session, when the final approval of *Dignitatis Humanae* would finally come.

CHAPTER FOUR

OVERCOMING THE OPPOSITION
AT THE COUNCIL

THE BISHOPS AND THEOLOGIANS actively desirous of putting the Second Vatican Council on record with a statement of the Church's developed teaching on religious freedom were generally well aware that the task would not be either automatic or easy, especially considering how the question had been tradition-ally formulated and stated in Church thinking. The initial state of mind of many of the bishops on the question was also not imme-diately favorable. The very first reading of the religious freedom *schema* independently of its initial appearance as a chapter in the ecumenism *schema*, of which it had originally been a part, came on November 23, 1963, near the end of the second session. On that occasion Bishop Émile de Smedt of Bruges, Belgium, who served throughout the Council as the *relator* of the *schema* — or what we Americans would call the "floor manager" of the measure — de-livered an illuminating and memorable address in which he laid out all the major arguments and substantive points which the Council was being asked to consider and approve. This address of Bishop de Smedt's was fundamentally important in laying out the case for religious freedom in a way that enabled the Council Fathers to see that what was being proposed was not contrary to traditional

Catholic teaching, but rather supplemented and developed it in an important way.

The basic points enumerated by Bishop de Smedt remained essentially unchanged through all the conciliar debates, the maneuvering, the many revisions (which mostly concerned how what the bishops said they wanted could best be presented), and, finally, the voting on the *schema* itself. It is worth citing some of the clarifications which Bishop de Smedt gave at the outset of the debates as to why the Council needed to issue the Declaration. It is particularly important to note the Belgian prelate's careful distinctions as to exactly what "religious liberty" meant in the text and context of the Declaration as a whole. Bishop de Smedt explained that:

> The term "religious liberty" has a definite meaning in our text. In the forthcoming discussion, great confusion might arise if any of the Fathers give to the expression a meaning that differs from the one intended by the text.
>
> When religious liberty is defended, it is not asserted that it is proper for man to consider the religious problem according to his own whim without any moral obligation, and decide for himself according to his own will whether or not to embrace religion (religious indifferentism).
>
> Nor is it affirmed that the human conscience is free in the sense that it is as it were outside the law, absolved from any obligation towards God (laicism).
>
> Nor is it said that falsehood is to be considered on an equal footing with truth, as though there were no objective norms of truth (doctrinal relativism).
>
> Nor is it admitted that man in any way has a quasi-right to maintain a peaceful complacency in the midst of uncertainty (dilettantistic pessimism).
>
> What, therefore, is meant in the text by "religious liberty"? Positively, religious liberty is the right of the human person

to the free exercise of religion according to the dictates of his conscience. Negatively, it is immunity from all external force in his personal relations with God.

These, then, were the major clarifications provided by Bishop Émile de Smedt of Bruges, Belgium, on the meaning of religious freedom as it would be affirmed in *Dignitatis Humanae*. His careful distinctions here were surely necessary if the whole question of religious freedom was to be put into its proper context; they were also influential in persuading many of the bishops who may have been doubtful or on the fence on the issue. If Bishop de Smedt was correct in identifying what the necessary distinctions which had to be made were, then it could easily be seen that what was being proposed in the document was fully in accord with traditional Church teaching.

The conservative opponents of the religious liberty *schema*, however, were insisting that what was being proposed did contradict past Church magisterial teachings. Archbishop Lefebvre expressly stated that the proposed Declaration contradicted the teachings of Pope Gregory XVI and Blessed Pope Pius IX. This has continued to be a claim of the Lefebvrists.

Moreover, in the years following the Council, prominent dissenting theologians on the left such as Gregory Baum, Charles Curran, Hans Küng, Daniel Maguire, and Richard McBrien have all repeated this same charge, and all have instanced the "changes" they saw in the Church's teaching on religious freedom in the Declaration as a justification for their own revisionist and dissenting positions. If the Church could change her teaching on religious freedom, they asked, pertinently, why could she not change other teachings of hers as well? Father Charles Curran, for instance, specifically offered this argument during a press conference in 1968 in defense of his public dissent from Pope Paul VI's encyclical *Humanae Vitae*. Nor would he have been wrong *if* the Church *had* changed her teaching when issuing the Declaration on Religious Freedom.

Similarly, Daniel Maguire, who like a number of other renegade theologians went on to deny the Church's teaching on the immorality of killing by abortion, wrote in a book edited by Father Curran that "Gregory XVI and Pius IX both condemned notions of religious liberty and freedom of conscience later to be blessed in Vatican II." Juan Luis Segundo, objecting to the Holy See's censure of certain elements of "liberation theology" was another theologian who insisted that *Dignitatis Humanae* had overturned the teaching of Blessed Pope Pius IX in the latter's *Syllabus of Errors*.

Whether or not the Church's magisterium *did* contradict itself in issuing this Declaration, however, remains the pertinent question — and it is too important a question to leave unexamined and unresolved. We therefore need to address the question. Why, then, indeed, did the opponents of the Declaration think they had a case when contending that it represented a change in the Church's previous constant teaching? We may perhaps begin to understand the concern behind such an allegation if we turn to some of the pronouncements of nineteenth-century popes on the subject of "freedom of religion" (or "freedom of conscience") and on what these popes taught on the subject of the duties of the State towards Almighty God and the true religion, namely, the Catholic religion.

In an 1832 encyclical entitled *Mirari Vos*, for example, Pope Gregory XVI roundly condemned what he called "the absurd and wrong view, or rather insanity [*deliramentum*], according to which freedom of conscience must be asserted and vindicated for everybody." His successor, Blessed Pope Pius IX, in his encyclical *Qui Pluribus* issued in 1846, similarly included among errors against the faith the notion that "there is no difference between religions," and also the position holding that "men can attain to eternal salvation by the practice of any religion whatever."

In 1864, the same Blessed Pope Pius IX issued his encyclical *Quanta Cura*, to which was attached his famous *Syllabus of Errors* — a summary listing of some of the common errors of the day against the faith which had been explicitly condemned by this pope in various encyclicals, allocutions, and other documents of his. The *Syllabus of Errors* created a veritable sensation throughout Europe in its day, and it has been invidiously quoted ever since — down to our own day — in order to convict the Catholic Church of reactionary, retrograde, and head-in-the-sand unreality, as well as of illiberality and authoritarianism. For many the *Syllabus* has been considered Exhibit A in the modern liberal case against the Church. Among the "errors" condemned by the pope in the *Syllabus*, for example, are the following:

> Every man is free to embrace and profess that religion which, guided by the light of reason, he shall consider true (15).
>
> In the present day it is no longer expedient that the Catholic religion should be held as the only religion of the State, to the exclusion of all other forms of worship (77).
>
> It has been wisely decided by law, in some Catholic countries, that persons coming to reside therein shall enjoy the public exercise of their own peculiar worship (78).

Remember: these propositions as well as some others in the same vein were *condemned* in the *Syllabus* as "errors" by the supreme teaching authority of the Church, Blessed Pope Pius IX. In the face of such definite and solemn pronouncements, how could Vatican Council II have ever gone on to teach that every human person nevertheless enjoys a right to religious freedom in public and in private? This was the question which the conservatives and traditionalists at the Council kept asking, and which not a few people continue to ask today. They are pertinent questions, and they certainly do need to be answered.

The successor of Blessed Pius IX, Pope Leo XIII, delivered himself of a number of similar pronouncements, which nobody who believes in the supreme teaching authority of the bishop of Rome in the Catholic Church can afford to pass over lightly. In his encyclical *Libertas Praestantissimum* on Human Liberty issued in 1888, for example, Leo XIII taught that the "chiefest and holiest" duty of every human person is to "worship God with devotion and piety." What Leo styled "liberty of worship,"

> ...if considered in relation to the State, clearly implies that there is no reason why the State should offer any homage to God, or should desire any public recognition of Him; that no one form of worship is to be preferred to another, but that all stand on an equal footing, no account being taken of the religion of the people, even if they profess the Catholic faith. But to justify this, it must needs be taken as true that the State has no duties towards God, or that such duties, if they exist, can be abandoned with impunity, both of which assertions are manifestly *false* (LP 21; emphasis added).

Again, in his encyclical *Immortale Dei* on the Christian Constitution of States issued in 1885, Leo XIII taught even more emphatically that:

> to hold... that there is no difference in matters of religion between forms that are unlike each other, and even contrary to each other, most clearly leads in the end to the rejection of all religion in both theory and practice. And this is the same thing as atheism, however it may differ from it in name. Men who really believe in the existence of God must, in order to be consistent with themselves and to avoid absurd conclusions, understand

that differing modes of divine worship involving dissimi-
larity and conflict even on most important points cannot all be equally probable, equally good, and equally
acceptable to God (ID 31).

Many other strong statements in the same vein from the same
nineteenth-century popes can be adduced to the same end. Those
we have quoted are merely examples. Moreover, these and similar
papal statements were brought out and quoted during the debates
on the religious freedom *schema* during the Council. The Council
Fathers were hardly ignorant of them, yet only a small minority of
them remained convinced that these papal statements precluded
the approval and issuance of *Dignitatis Humanae*. How were the
apparent contradictions created by these nineteenth-century papal
teachings resolved in the minds of the Council Fathers in such a
way that an overwhelming majority of them eventually voted to
approve the Declaration?

We have already quoted above from the key 1963 Council
speech of Belgian Bishop Émile de Smedt, the *relator* of the religious freedom *schema* at the Council, in which he laid out the
general lines of the issue and pointed out how the *meaning* of the
term "religious liberty" in the conciliar text did not, in fact, *include*
the things singled out by the nineteenth-century popes and specifically condemned by them — things such as religious indifferentism,
doctrinal relativism, or laicism (which English-speakers would
normally call "secularism"). In the Declaration as approved by
the Council Fathers, religious freedom means, simply and solely,
according to Bishop de Smedt's explanation, "positively... the right
of the human person to the free exercise of religion according to
the dictates of his conscience. Negatively, it is immunity from all
external force."

Bishop de Smedt went on in his speech to show specifically
that when Gregory XVI or Pius IX condemned what they called

"freedom of conscience," they were condemning "the ideology of the rationalists who founded their conclusions upon the principle that the individual conscience is under no law." "Freedom of worship" was similarly condemned by the nineteenth-century popes when "based on religious indifferentism." Again, the separation of the Church from the State was condemned when it was "based on the rationalistic principle of the juridical omni-competence of the State, according to which the Church is to be incorporated into the monistic organism of the State and be subjected to its supreme authority."

"To understand these condemnations correctly," Bishop de Smedt concluded, "we must see in them the constant doctrine and solicitude of the Church concerning the true dignity of the human person and his true liberty.... For the ultimate basis of human dignity lies in the fact that man is a creature of God. He is not God himself but an image of God." And, of course, "the dignity of the human person" is the principle on which the entire Declaration on Religious Freedom is based. Far from contradicting the teachings of the earlier popes, the Declaration represents a doctrinal *development* in a different direction from the preoccupations of the nineteenth century of the same basic principles on which the popes of that day were also operating. In other words, the Declaration was *addressing a different problem* than the ones the nineteenth-century popes were concerned with. What those popes taught about the dangers of religious indifferentism, secularism, relativism, and the like, as well as about the duties of man and the State towards God the Creator, was true then, and remains true now (if only someone, somehow, as far as the latter duties are concerned, could just get modern man today to *recognize* his duties towards his Creator!).

The Declaration itself recognizes the truth of these nineteenth-century papal teachings when it states that "it leaves untouched traditional Catholic teaching on the moral duty of individuals and societies towards the true religion and toward the one Church of Christ." In fact, the Declaration does more than just leave these teachings untouched; it positively affirms that "all men are bound to seek the truth, especially in what concerns God and his Church, and to embrace the truth they come to know, and to hold fast to it" (DH 1).

In spite of the Declaration's own affirmations of the very papal teachings otherwise used by the traditionalists to question its own validity and authenticity as Catholic doctrine, then, the Council Fathers, in approving it, were fully cognizant of another line of papal teaching. This is the series of developments beginning with Pope Leo XIII himself (in the very encyclicals quoted against *Dignitatis Humanae* by opponents of the Declaration), which pointed towards the affirmations of religious freedom that finally emerged full-blown in Pope John XXIII's *Pacem in Terris* before finally being enshrined in the Vatican II Declaration on Religious Freedom. The Council Fathers should have been fully cognizant of these developments all along — for the simple reason that Bishop de Smedt laid them all out in his key 1963 address to the Council Fathers assembled in St. Peter's, and showed how they accorded with traditional Catholic teaching. The traditionalist attacks on *Dignitatis Humanae* that came after the Council failed to take into account that both the arguments and the texts they adduced against the Declaration had all been thoroughly aired and discussed at the Council before the Declaration on Religious Freedom was finally voted.

In *Immortale Dei*, for example, Leo XIII had distinguished between the Church as the people of God and civil society as a separate community, and thus he had laid the groundwork for the affirmation of a right of freedom from external coercion in the latter, that is, in civil society. In *Libertas Praestantissimum*, the same pope taught plainly that "modern freedoms" could be "tolerated": this, indeed, was one of the doctrinal bases for the idea that "error" could be "tolerated," even though it had no "rights" as such. Nevertheless, this granting of tolerance represented an idea capable of development in another direction. And this development was what was going to take place at Vatican II.

Pope Pius XI, in his 1931 encyclical *Non Abbiamo Bisogno* directed against the Italian Fascists, introduced an important distinction by continuing to condemn "freedom of conscience" (singular) as implying freedom from being subject to the moral law of God. At the same time, Pius XI declared that he would joyfully fight for "freedom of consciences" (plural) from external coercion, especially coercion by the State. In his 1937 encyclical *Mit Brennender Sorge* directed against the Nazis, the same pope taught that "man as a person possesses God-given rights which must remain immune from all denial, privation, or interference on the part of society." Or, again, in the same encyclical he insisted that "the believer possesses the inalienable right to profess his faith and practice it.... Laws which interfere with or render difficult this profession and practice are in contradiction to the natural law."

In other words, responding to the totalitarianisms of the day, Pope Pius XI was already teaching a concept of religious freedom (freedom from coercion) very like the concept Vatican II would adopt in *Dignitatis Humanae*. Similarly, Pope Pius XII, in a radio message broadcast on December 24, 1942, affirmed among "the fundamental rights of the person... the right to private and public worship of God." This was only one of a number of similar affirmations of the same kind included in the wartime radio messages and other addresses of Pius XII (one of which was quoted earlier). And we also saw earlier how Blessed John XXIII affirmed the same thing in his encyclical *Pacem et Terris*.

All of these teachings should have been known to the bishops debating religious liberty at Vatican II, because Bishop de Smedt quoted these and similar passages from the papal writings in his foundational 1963 address. Most of the Council Fathers were thus fully aware of them when they voted for *Dignitatis Humanae*: they were thus approving no "new," previously unheard-of Church doctrine. Rather, they were approving in the Declaration an entirely legitimate development of what amounted to a considerable body of previous papal teachings.

In one sense, no Church teaching is more traditional than the teaching that the human person must be free from coercion in matters of religious belief. As far back as the Second Council of Nicaea (the Church's seventh ecumenical council) in the year 987, we find this council legislating that Jews should be free to worship "openly according to their own religion." In his *Summa Theologica*, Saint Thomas Aquinas similarly held that "among the infidels there are some who have never adopted the Christian faith, such as Gentiles and Jews, and these should in no way be constrained to embrace the faith and profess belief. For belief depends upon the will" (*ST* II-II, q.10, a.8). *Dignitatis Humanae* surely echoed this point made by St. Thomas Aquinas when it taught that "the truth cannot impose itself except by virtue of its own truth, as it makes its entrance into the mind at once quietly and with power" (DH 1).

Contrary to past and present claims of some traditionalists, then, the teaching enshrined in Vatican II's Declaration on Religious Freedom is eminently traditional and entirely in accord with the Catholic tradition — and does not in any way contradict past teachings of the Church's magisterium. It is no surprise, in fact, that Pope John Paul II, who as Archbishop Karol Wojtyla championed the Declaration on Religious Freedom so firmly during the Council, should have invoked the same Declaration so prominently in the very first encyclical of his pontificate, namely, his 1979 encyclical *Redemptor Hominis* on the Redeemer of Man. In this encyclical, the Polish pope wrote that:

> The Declaration on Religious Freedom shows us convincingly that, when Christ and, after him, his apostles

proclaimed the truth that comes not from men but from God — "My teaching is not mine but his who sent me" (Jn 7:16), that is, the Father's — they preserved, while acting with their full force of spirit, a deep esteem for man, for his intellect, his will, his freedom. Thus, the human person's dignity itself becomes part of the content of that proclamation, being included not necessarily in words but by an attitude towards it. This attitude seems to fit the special needs of our times. Since man's true freedom is not found in everything that the various systems and individuals see and propagate as freedom, the Church, because of her divine mission becomes all the more the guardian of this freedom, which is the condition and basis for the human person's true dignity (RH 12).

Further on in the same encyclical, Pope John Paul II again quoted the Vatican II Declaration and declared that:

the curtailment of the religious freedom of individuals and communities is not only a painful experience, but it is above all an attack on man's dignity and his objective rights.... We are undoubtedly confronted here with a radical injustice with regard to what is particularly deep within man, what is authentically human.... It is difficult, even from a "purely human" point of view, to accept a position that gives only atheism the right of citizenship in public and social life, while believers are, as though by principle, barely tolerated, or are treated as second-class citizens, or are even — and this has already happened — entirely deprived of the rights of citizenship (RH 17).

Like the Second Vatican Council itself, then, Pope John Paul

II saw in this Declaration on Religious Freedom a necessary bulwark raised up by the Church against the particular tyrannies and totalitarianisms of the modern world. In spite of all the controversy that surrounded the Declaration during the Council, and still surrounds it today in some circles, Vatican II surely acted both truly and aptly in issuing it. And once the Council had approved it, and the reigning pontiff, Pope Paul VI, had ratified it, the Declaration then necessarily took its place among the authentic acts of the Church's extraordinary magisterium, and thus became a permanent part of the Church's doctrinal legacy as well as binding upon the Catholic faithful.

CHAPTER FIVE

THE CONTENTS OF THE DECLARATION
ON RELIGIOUS FREEDOM

I N THE COURSE OF DISCUSSING its origins and development at the Second Vatican Council, we have already gotten more than a glimpse of the contents of *Dignitatis Humanae*. It is both a short and a not very complicated document that was intended to serve a very specific purpose. Nevertheless, it is worth reviewing its high points even at the risk of some repetition. No Vatican II document remains more pertinent to the situation of the Church today — especially when we consider the situation of religious freedom in the world today.

The text of *Dignitatis Humanae* begins with an introductory section that invokes the importance of the human dignity from which the Declaration takes its Latin title. As we have noted, the subject of human dignity was one of the major themes of the Second Vatican Council. Typical of the times, as was also the case, especially, with the Council's Pastoral Constitution on the Church in the Modern World, *Gaudium et Spes*, is the assertion in the first sentence that "contemporary man" insists on "responsible freedom" and rejects "coercion," as well as demanding that "constitutional limits should be set on the powers of government" (DH 1). In this case, the Council seems inclined to go along with "contemporary man." Far from seeing the State as in any sense an upholder of

Christianity or the Catholic faith, *Dignitatis Humanae* sees it as a source of possible oppression. The bishops at the Council no doubt had in mind the recent experiences of both Fascist and Nazi totalitarianisms in Italy and Germany, and, of course, Communist totalitarianism was still going strong in the Eastern Bloc of nations under the sway of the Soviet Union at the time of the Council.

The twin themes of the dignity of the human person and the necessity for legal and constitutional limits on the power of the State to coerce really constitute the primary basis for everything else that the document says concerning the free practice of religion.

A short introductory section then makes mention both of the truth revealed by God to his Church and the Church's commission to "make disciples of all nations" (Mt 28:19). *Dignitatis Humanae* will conclude, of course, with its famous passage identifying the Church as "the teacher of truth" (DH 14). But here at the outset the text pertinently declares that "all men are bound to seek the truth" (DH 1). Nevertheless, it also recognizes what we have already noted, namely, that "truth cannot impose itself except by virtue of its own truth, as it makes its entrance into the mind at once quietly and with power" (*Ibid.*). Thus, truth itself can never be imposed or coerced even though it *is* true.

Precisely because all men are bound to seek and embrace the truth — for the simple reason that it is God's truth — left untouched and intact in the document, and necessarily so, is what the text calls "the traditional Catholic doctrine on the moral duty of men and societies toward the true religion and toward the one Church of Christ" (*Ibid.*). How individuals or societies should or might be persuaded to recognize this moral duty of theirs is another question entirely, of course, and this is *not* what *Dignitatis Humanae* is about; it simply reiterates the fact that there is a moral duty towards the true religion, which is understood by the document to be the Catholic religion.

Before launching into the substance of their message, though, the Council Fathers, significantly, as we have already noted, decided to state very clearly at the beginning their intention "to *develop* the doctrine of recent popes on the inviolable rights of the human person and the constitutional order of society" (*Ibid.*; emphasis added). It is rare that magisterial statements of the Church state explicitly in this fashion that they do, in fact, represent a "development of doctrine." The Declaration's short introductory section is followed by two chapters, one on the General Principle of Religious Freedom (Nos. 2-8) and one on Religious Freedom in the Light of Revelation (Nos. 9-15).

We have already seen how the Declaration affirms in its first chapter that human persons have a right to religious liberty based upon their inherent human dignity; that this right essentially consists of freedom from coercion; that it should be legally and constitutionally protected as a civil right; and that the only limitations upon it should be the just requirements of the public order. But since "the right to religious freedom has its foundation not in the subjective disposition of the person, but in his very [human] *nature*," this right belongs even to "those who do not live up to their obligation of seeking the truth and adhering to it" (DH 2; emphasis added). In other words, even those who are in error retain their right to be free from coercion. This, of course, was a major sticking point for the opponents of the Declaration at the Council; what they understood was that error had no rights, and the truth that human beings did have rights, even the right to be free from coercion when wrong, was not persuasive for many of them.

Father John Courtney Murray, S.J., however, observed very pertinently in this connection that no one truly does have "a right to believe what is false or do what is wrong," but only a right to be free from coercion. "It is worth noting," Father Murray added in his commentary on *Dignitatis Humanae* found in the Abbott edition of the Council's documents, "that the Declaration does not base

the right to the free exercise of religion on 'freedom of conscience.'
Nowhere does this phrase occur. And the Declaration nowhere
lends its authority to the theory for which the phrase frequently
stands, namely, that I have the right to do what my conscience tells
me to do, simply because my conscience tells me to do it. This is
a perilous theory. Its particular peril is subjectivism — the notion
that, in the end, it is my conscience which determines what is right
or wrong, true or false." Father Murray would not live to see the
day when many theologians, including many of his fellow Jesuits,
would join dissenting theologians in the Church nearly everywhere
in assuring Catholic married couples that their consciences *could*
decide contrary to the objective truth as found in the teaching of the
Church; and since then some Catholic theologians have erroneously
attempted to hold that we can indeed in conscience decide other
questions contrary to what the teaching of the Church enjoins.

Dignitatis Humanae, however, countenanced no such error. While it repeated the long established truth that we may not,
morally, act contrary to our consciences, it also reiterated the
necessarily related truth that conscience must always be formed
in accordance with objective truth — which the document itself
consistently equates with the teaching of the Church.

It was fully realized that the freedom from coercion enjoyed
by individuals logically also had to be extended to men "when they
act in community.... Provided the just demands of the public order
are observed, religious communities rightfully claim freedom in order that they may govern themselves according to their own norms"
(DH 4). In other words, non-Catholics have the right — and would
have it even in a theoretically "Catholic" state or commonwealth
— to practice their non-Catholic religion publicly and as a community. Such a right pertaining to whole communities, of course,
was generally not so explicitly recognized in the old Catholic confessional states, where the Catholic Church was the established
Church — any more than the freedom of Catholic worship was

recognized in kingdoms or countries where a non-Catholic Church was established, such as England or the Scandinavian countries.

The phrase, "the just demands of the public order," is encountered several times in the text. Both during the Council and since, this concept has been criticized as falling short of the traditional Catholic idea of "the common good." And why indeed should not the common good be the basis on which religious liberty might legitimately be subject to some limitations? Serious questions would seem to arise today when, for example, Wiccans ("witches") make public claims to be recognized as "ministers of religion" — say, in the military services so that they would presumably have to be provided chaplains. The same kinds of questions arise when cults engaging in animal sacrifice or drug use make similar claims. And such problems would seem to be particularly acute today in the case of religions preaching a violent form of *jihad* or its equivalent to their adherents. On what principled basis can the public authorities legitimately suppress or restrict such religions, cults, or activities? Do "the just demands of the public order" provide a sufficiently principled basis?

Dignitatis Humanae does not provide a completely clear answer to this question. Yet it was only after considerable discussion, as it was also contrary to the wishes of many of the Council Fathers, that the conciliar commission drafters of the Declaration finally did approve the concept of "the public order" rather than "the common good." They did so because, it was said, they did not *want* to grant to Communist governments, for example, the right to decide what constituted "the common good." Today the same principle must surely be applied to secularist governments operating in "the naked public square" made famous by the late Father Richard John Neuhaus. For such governments as even the current United States government, for example, the "common good" can unfortunately now include at the present time such things as no-fault divorce and abortion on demand as well as government-funded Medicaid abortions for the poor or "comprehensive" classroom sex education expressly designed to initiate children into the sexual revolution by demonstrating the use of condoms and such. In some American states, the common good already now includes so-called "same-sex marriage," and we are already in a situation in some of these states where belief or advocacy of Catholic (or biblical) teaching on the immorality of homosexual acts is stigmatized and may soon be outlawed.

Once governments have abandoned the moral law of God in these matters, as is true of many if not most governments today, they surely *cannot* serve any longer as the proper arbiters or defin-ers of "the common good." Once again, Vatican II was prescient in this regard. The problem here is the same as the problem encoun-tered by those who, hearkening back to the confessional States in "Catholic" countries, where the State once did (after a fashion!) uphold the truths of the faith and its accompanying morality with the instruments of its State power, continue to hold that the State *ought* to uphold the truths of Christ's faith — and enforce its moral rules.

This is no doubt true in one sense: in abstract theory, the State *ought* indeed to uphold God's truth and God's law. But if the State itself no longer recognizes this truth or this law, or accepts any responsibility for them, as is the case today — or, as is increas-ingly also the case today, even itself *sponsors* immorality and what Pope Benedict XVI at the time of his election to the chair of Peter accurately styled "the dictatorship of relativism" — then the idea that it is the State that ought to uphold Catholic truth and moral-ity becomes an entirely theoretical and idealistic position, with no relation to the reality of how today's typical secular States think and operate. The Council Fathers may not even have consciously had all this in mind when they approved *Dignitatis Humanae* in its final form, but today we can clearly see here that, once again, the Council Fathers decided perhaps better than they knew.

In any case, the Council Fathers were evidently prepared to take the risk of allowing some loopholes in the interests of establishing the general principle of freedom from coercion in matters of religious belief and practice. *Dignitatis Humanae* is neither a perfect document nor a completely comprehensive one anyway, nor does it claim to be such. Its declared aim was deliberately limited to upholding religious freedom from coercion as a civil right; it did not attempt to settle all outstanding Church-State issues. Further developments in the Church's teaching on both religious freedom and Church-State relations are possible and perhaps even likely. But since the Declaration holds that religious liberty is a *civil* right, it surely constitutes a right that should be upheld by public authorities everywhere. The Declaration thus states: "The protection and promotion of the inviolable rights of man rank among the essential duties of government" (DH 6). Further on, the text explicitly specifies that freedom should be respected and curtailed only when and insofar as is necessary and also that civil authorities must act in accordance with "juridical norms which are in accordance with the objective moral order" (DH 7). Here again this is no doubt easier said than it is to get modern governments to act in this manner; yet what the document specifies is probably as much as could reasonably be demanded by the Church, especially in the moral climate that unhappily prevails in our modern post-Christian society today.

In spite of its generally new approach to some old issues, though, the Declaration still does recognize the possibility — and legitimacy in its proper sphere — of the older concept of a "confessional State" with an "established" Church or religion. At the same time, however, it holds that minority religions in such States should enjoy legal recognition and respect along with the established Church: "If, in view of peculiar circumstances obtaining among people, special civil recognition is given to one religious community in the constitutional order of society, it is at the same time imperative that the right of all citizens and religious communities to religious freedom should be recognized and made effective in practice" (DH 6). This, again, does represent a change from the practice of some of the former confessional States. In his notes on *Dignitatis Humanae*, Father John Courtney Murray observed that, in his opinion, "the Council wished to insinuate that establishment, at least from the Catholic point of view, is a matter of historical circumstance, not *theological doctrine*" (emphasis added).

Father Murray could and perhaps should have added that this was not always recognized by Catholics, as the conciliar debates surely proved. Such a principle would never have been allowed, for example, by some of the concordats under which the Catholic Church once operated in a number of countries, including even countries such as the Spain of the dictator Francisco Franco. But then the same principle would have applied to those countries with established Churches which once persecuted or marginalized Catholics, such as Protestant England or Lutheran Scandinavia up until very recent times.

Today we should take note of how the principle could still apply to, say, the Chaldean Catholic Church in contemporary Iraq, not to speak of other countries with Buddhist, Hindu, or Muslim majorities, where the Catholic Church sometimes labors under enormous disabilities, if she is not actually outlawed. The mutual toleration and respect that *Dignitatis Humanae* sanctions, even while the Catholic Church continues to claim possession of the fullness of God's revealed truth, is a principle that would serve very well in modern Islamic States which claim to be seeking to establish "democracy," for example, but which seem unable to deal with the fact of religious pluralism. The Russian Orthodox Church too, which continues to claim a religious monopoly in its "territory" — while enjoying the freedom in Western countries to organize to serve its emigrant congregations — might well consider the same principle to a greater extent than it has up to now. Many other examples of the same kind could be cited.

The Catholic Church in *Dignitatis Humanae* has shown how a religion claiming to possess and propagate absolute truth can nevertheless try to live in peace and relative harmony with those among whom she finds herself, who not only do not agree with her claims but who may actually be opposed to them. The key requirement here is respect for the *human dignity* of all, no matter what their beliefs may be. This is a principle that has not been widely respected in human history — far from it — but it is a valid principle nonetheless, which the Second Vatican Council was both prescient and wise to pursue and develop in the way that it did in this Declaration. The Catholic Church can now be confident that she possesses a firm principled basis on which to affirm religious freedom.

In its second chapter, dealing with religious liberty in the light of revelation, *Dignitatis Humanae* is anxious to show that the doctrine of religious liberty which it expounds "has roots in divine revelation." The text grants that "revelation does not affirm in so many words the right of man to immunity from external coercion in matters religious," but it does nevertheless "disclose the dignity of the human person in its full dimensions" (DH 9). If indeed human dignity is the basis for the right to religious liberty, then that dignity is abundantly grounded in revelation. Moreover, "it is one of the major tenets of Catholic doctrine that man's response to God in faith must be *free*" (DH 10; emphasis added). The text immediately adds that nobody "is to be forced to embrace the Christian faith against his will" (*Ibid.*). Therefore, as Father John Courtney Murray, again, explains:

> The unwavering Christian dogma that the act of Christian faith must be a free response to the Word and grace of God reveals the divine respect for human freedom and for man's inalienable responsibility

toward the direction of his own life. The constitutional
principle of religious freedom is not a conclusion from
this Christian dogma. The connection is rather more
historical. That is to say, given the Christian doctrine
of the freedom of faith, men would gradually come —
as over the centuries they have come — to realize that
man's religious life is an affair of responsible freedom,
from which all coercion is to be excluded. Given this
Christian appreciation of the value of freedom (and
given also the growing secular experience of freedom as
a social value and a political end), men could not fail to
become increasingly conscious that religious freedom is
an exigency of the dignity of the person, as this dignity
is disclosed by the revelation that man is made in the
image of God. Moreover, experience would also make
it clear that, where religious freedom prevails, a climate
of freedom is created in society which itself favors the
free preaching of the Gospel and the free living of the
Christian life.

In the sense that Father Murray explains here, the principle
of religious liberty surely is, then, rooted in revelation. The text
goes on at some length citing numerous scriptural passages to show
that coercion in religious matters is in any case also contrary to the
spirit of the Gospels. *Dignitatis Humanae* claims that the Church
is simply being faithful "to the truth of the Gospel" and is "following the way of Christ and the apostles when she recognizes and
give support to the principle of religious freedom as befitting the
dignity of man and as being in accord with divine revelation" (DH
12). The text even boasts of how the Church through the ages "has
kept safe and handed on the doctrine received from the Master and
the apostles." But there is also a frank admission that "in the life
of the People of God as it has made its pilgrim way through the

vicissitudes of human history, there has at times appeared a way of acting that was hardly in accord with the spirit of the Gospel or even opposed to it" (DH 12).

In other words, in spite of her constant teaching in opposition to coercion, the Church at various times in her history nevertheless either countenanced the coercive institutions of the State in the supposed interests of religion, or even on more than a few occasions resorted to them herself. This is a rare admission of fault which the Church, like so many other institutions, does not find easy to acknowledge — though the Council Fathers obviously considered it necessary in this case. We should take note here, though, of the shift in the text from "the Church" to "the People [of God]" — in line with the traditional doctrine that the Church herself, as the Bride of Christ, is sinless, even while her "children" are both capable of, and too often guilty of, sin.

However, this admission of the past sins of Catholics, including churchmen, is brief, general, and deliberately understated in this text. Nevertheless it is real and sincere. With the enactment of *Dignitatis Humanae*, the Church went firmly on the record stating her fixed intention henceforth to renounce in principle the use of coercive measures. Thus, Vatican II itself can be credited with the idea of expressing regret for the past sins of the children of the Church — a theme which Pope John Paul II would greatly stress, especially later in his pontificate, and which Pope Benedict XVI would repeat.

Two other aspects of the Church's teaching in *Dignitatis Humanae* must be mentioned. The first is that the Church herself must enjoy the religious freedom which she is espousing in the document. The text is quite emphatic about this:

> Among the things that concern the good of the Church and indeed the welfare of society here on earth — things therefore that are always and everywhere to be kept se-

cure and defended against all injury — this certainly is
pre-eminent, namely that the Church should enjoy that
full measure of freedom which her care for the salvation
of men requires. This is a sacred freedom because the
only-begotten Son endowed with it the Church which
He purchased with His blood. Indeed, it is so much the
property of the Church that to act against it is to act
against the will of God. The freedom of the Church is
the fundamental principle in what concerns the relations
between the Church and governments and the whole
civil order (DH 13).

Just as the Church calls for religious freedom for man and
societies, then, she calls for the same freedom for herself. This is
an eminently traditional position which the Church has claimed
since her foundation. It is based, *inter alia*, upon the principle,
coming from the lips of the Lord Jesus Christ himself, that it is
necessary to "render to Caesar the things that are Caesar's, and
to God the things that are God's" (Mt 22:21; Mk 12:17; Lk 22:25).
The Church has to be free if she is to be able to carry out properly
her God-given task dedicated to the sanctification and salvation of
all men and women. In the course of her long history, the Church
has often had to *fight* to preserve this freedom, and the historical
record shows that she has rarely in the end failed to fight when
necessary, especially against repressive governments seeking to
control her. In many periods of history, the Church has *had* to fight
for her freedom — so great has been the temptation on the part
of the State in nearly every historical period to control such an
important and influential entity as the Church has proved herself
to be in every age.

It was Father John Courtney Murray, again, in his foundational 1960 book *We Hold These Truths: Catholic Reflections on the
American Proposition*, who pointed out how the Church's efforts

in history to maintain her own freedom helped contribute to the freedom and pluralism which the world today claims to value so highly. Fr. Murray wrote in this regard:

> It is an historical commonplace to say that the essential political effect of Christianity was to destroy the classical view of society as a single homogenous structure, within which the political power stood forth as the representative of society both in its religious and in its political aspects. Augustus was both *Summus Imperator* and *Pontifex Maximus*; the *ius divinum* was simply part of the *ius civile*; and outside the empire there was no civil society but only barbarism. The new Christian view was based on a radical distinction between the order of the sacred and the order of the secular: "Two there are, august Emperor, by which the world is ruled on title of original and sovereign right — the consecrated authority of the priesthood and the royal power." In this celebrated sentence of Gelasius I, written to the Byzantine Emperor Anastasius I in 494 A.D., the emphasis laid on the word "two" bespoke the revolutionary character of the Christian dispensation.

However, the pluralism inherent in the recognition of more than one source of authority in society is in continual danger of breaking down in the face of the pressures from the State. This is especially true of the modern secular State which is so prone to claim omni-competence. Threats to the Church's freedom have hardly disappeared today — on the contrary. We need think, for example, only of the ongoing efforts of the government of Communist China to control the activities of the Church in that country. Nor is it the only government that strives to do this. Even in some modern democracies, secularist and secularizing governments continue to

try to dictate to the Church what can and cannot (without consequences) be taught to and enjoined upon the faithful. We need
think only in this regard of the saying of that old Radical Socialist
French politician, Georges Clemenceau, who turned the Christian
principle on its head when he claimed that it was necessary to
"render to Caesar the things that are Caesar's — and everything
is Caesar's"! This is not any exaggeration of the way many people
think in today's radically secularized society. They see no reason
to grant the Church's freedom to be herself. Vatican II's *Dignitatis Humanae* thus must stand as one of the Church's considered
answers to such secularizing tendencies and pressures.

As we near the end of this conciliar document, another
traditional teaching found in *Dignitatis Humanae* must be noted,
however, and it is one of the most important teachings of all. Indeed, it is more than just another claim of the Church's. Rather, it
is a principle which the Church has consistently both insisted upon
and *acted upon* throughout virtually her entire history. Vatican II's
Declaration on Religious Freedom admirably stated this principle
as a now permanent feature of the Church's extraordinary magisterium: it is the claim that the Catholic Church is nothing less than
the appointed teacher of God's truth to mankind.

Just as the Second Vatican Council selected its Decree on
Ecumenism, *Unitatis Redintegratio*, as its chosen vehicle to reaffirm the Church's ancient and enduring claim to be "the one, true
Church" of Christ (see UR 3), so the Council selected this Declaration on Religious Freedom as its chosen vehicle to reaffirm
the equally ancient truths that the Church teaches both truly and
"with authority," just as Christ himself did (cf. Lk 4:32), and that
what the Church teaches, since it is true, is incumbent upon all men
everywhere to believe and act upon.

Yes: the document clearly specifies this, namely, that the
Church is the teacher of truth; and it specifies further that the be-
lieving faithful are bound to believe and put into practice in their

lives the truth that the Church teaches. This is one of the most important of all the teachings of the Second Vatican Council. It was always implicit in the Church's claim to be what she is; but the Council saw fit to make it quite explicit and unmistakable. We may fittingly conclude our examination of the content of this most important Council document by quoting the Declaration's own eloquent affirmation of it:

> In the formation of their consciences, the Christian faithful ought carefully to attend to the sacred and certain doctrine of the Church. For the Church is, by the will of Christ, the teacher of truth. It is her duty to give utterance to, and authoritatively to teach, that truth which is Christ himself, and also to declare and confirm by her authority those principles of the moral order which have their origins in human nature itself (DH 14)

The teacher of truth: This is what the Church says she is. It is what Christ — who told Pilate, "For this I was born, and for this I came into the world, to bear witness to the truth" (Jn 18:37) — himself said the Church would be when he conferred upon the apostles, whose successors are the Catholic bishops in communion with the bishop of Rome, the pope, the task of providing leadership in the Church down through history: "He who hears you, hears me, and he who rejects you, rejects me, and he who rejects me rejects the one who sent me" (Lk 10:16). This saying applies to the Church's hierarchy today, as it did to the apostles themselves at the time when it was first enunciated.

The Church, then, *has* to be the teacher of truth, since, as Christ indicated, she would be speaking for *him*. So it is no accident, then — nor should it be any surprise — that Vatican II here teaches that the faithful must form their consciences in accordance with the "sacred and certain doctrine of the Church." The Council was quite literal and quite serious about this, even while also declaring that there ought to be religious freedom for all.

In our own day, following the Council, and quite ironically, many people, in what became in the post-conciliar years a new era of widespread dissent from Catholic teaching, wrongly decided that what the Church teaches was not necessarily always the truth. Such people often remained in the Church, or claimed to. Presumably they continued to see the Church as an admirable and vital community — the world's largest social welfare organization as it were — among other things.

But she was no longer regarded by them as the teacher of truth. Contrary to the hopes and intentions of Vatican II, her teachings somehow came to be considered optional by many, affirmations they could supposedly pick and choose among as they saw fit. The "cafeteria Catholic" phenomenon became an unhappy widespread reality. The prominent Catholic politicians who were "personally opposed" to abortion while supporting and even promoting legalized abortion were perhaps among the most notorious of these new cafeteria Catholics. They precisely did *not* accept that the Catholic Church was the teacher of truth, as the Council had so clearly and prophetically specified. In this they were profoundly mistaken, of course, and they were also oddly at variance with the Council's plain teaching. Vatican II Catholics they were *not*, whatever they may have imagined.

We should not forget, then, that what the Council actually taught was that the Catholic Church *is* "the teacher of truth," and that the faithful are obliged to form their consciences in accordance with the truths that the Church teaches. These truths are nothing else but the truths of Jesus Christ himself. This is the real and proper content and message and legacy of *Dignitatis Humanae*.

CHAPTER SIX

SOME APPLICATIONS

THE CATHOLIC CHURCH makes a unique claim to be the channel of God's revelation to mankind. The Church claims to be the teacher of truth, no less, as Vatican II's *Dignitatis Humanae* pointedly affirmed and as we have now verified. For a very long time the Church's consciousness of being such a chosen vessel perhaps helped prevent the development of a clear teaching about how the Church and her faithful ought to deal with those who do not accept her claim, or who perhaps even promote incompatible, rival, and even contradictory claims of their own. The idea of religious freedom for all was not an idea that ever got easily and naturally developed in the course of human history. This was no doubt the case precisely *because* religions believe their teachings to be true. Since they also believe that truth is paramount, it seems to follow as a matter of common sense that "error has no rights"; rival beliefs need not necessarily be respected. Indeed it has been frequently and quite commonly thought that they should be suppressed, since they are by definition *not* true.

Even today — or, rather, especially today, by the secularly minded — it remains a very common and widespread opinion that true freedom is not even possible unless absolute truth claims are laid aside. To claim to possess truth is thought by many to require that freedom be denied in principle to those who do not accept that truth (especially whenever one has the power to enforce the truth claim in question). The Catholic Church, however, is unusual and perhaps even unique in affirming religious freedom for all, even while she continues to retain her claim to be the teacher of a truth that is absolute. This affirmation came about when the Church realized that the claims of human dignity — the dignity of beings created in the image of God — required respect for the conscientiously held religious beliefs of human beings even when they were mistaken, so long as the public order was preserved. At Vatican Council II the Church enshrined this principle in a Declaration that was given the very name "of human dignity," the Declaration on Religious Freedom, *Dignitatis Humanae*. This, of course, is the very Declaration that we have been concerned with in this book.

At the Council, a young German theological *peritus*, or advisor, Father Joseph Ratzinger, saw the debates on religious liberty and the document that issued from them as truly marking an epoch for the Church. Shortly after the Council ended, he wrote:

> The debate on religious liberty will in later years be considered one of the most important events of the Council already rich enough in important events. To use the catch-phrase once again, there was in St. Peter's the sense that here was the end of the Middle Ages, the end event of the Constantinian age.

For among other things, the Declaration marked and meant a new era when the Church would henceforth no longer be necessarily linked with the State and its set of priorities, which so often in history had provided the circumstances in which the imperatives of the Gospel could too easily get set aside or lost. As we have noted, Vatican II did not attempt to resolve the Church-State issue itself; but its Declaration on Religious Freedom did resolve the question of how religious belief itself should be treated — within the framework that, as we have seen, was so carefully laid out and explained in the document itself.

What the Second Vatican Council laid out in this relatively short but very pertinent document has now become part of the permanent legacy of Christ's Church. The Church cannot but teach and act upon the principles the Council provided. Probably in the nature of the case, though, *Dignitatis Humanae* did not inspire as many post-conciliar follow-up documents as some of the other documents of the Council. Actually, there was not all that much to add. The text is pretty clear and complete as it stands, at least for the present day. Moreover, the Church has sincerely tried to abide by it since the Council. And her efforts in that regard have had a notable effect on, e.g., ecumenism, to name only one subject. The Catholic Church can no longer be accused of having one set of rules where she is dominant or in the majority, and another set where her members constitute a minority.

From time to time in the post-conciliar era, the Church has also, importantly, invoked the principles of *Dignitatis Humanae*, especially in calling for respect for religious liberty in concrete cases, e.g., with respect to Communist China, as we have noted. Actually, the possible applications have been many, although as we indicated at the beginning, to go into the sometimes burning questions related to religious liberty today would get us into a very large subject and would take us beyond the scope of what this book has tried to accomplish. We can only mention an illustrative example or two here.

One notable instance, for example, where the Declaration contributed exactly what was needed in an important contemporary situation was the letter dated September 1, 1980, entitled "The Freedom of Conscience and Religion," which Pope John Paul II sent to the Heads of State of the countries which had signed the 1975 Helsinki Conference on European Security and Cooperation. This Helsinki Conference, of course, was one of the few relatively successful efforts undertaken in moderating the conflicts of the Cold War between the West and the Soviet Union. This came about in part because the Soviet Union had signed on to the Helsinki accords for its own reasons, but then once committed as a signatory, it found it hard to back away when called to account.

Pope John Paul II sent his letter on the Freedom of Conscience and Religion to all the Helsinki signatories in September, 1980, in connection with a follow-up meeting to the original Helsinki Conference that was taking place in Madrid, Spain. The pope's letter was practically a word-for-word repeat — with added elaboration — of *Dignitatis Humanae* itself, along with some of the points in Blessed John XXIII's encyclical *Pacem in Terris*. John Paul II's main purpose was to remind the Helsinki signatories of what they had committed themselves to. The pope's letter was widely and favorably commented on at the time.

Then, in December, 1980, when fears were running high that the Soviet Union might intervene militarily in Poland to put down the Solidarity labor movement there — there were credible reports that Soviet military units were being assembled for that purpose — the Polish pope addressed a strong letter to the Soviet leader Leonid Brezhnev reminding him of the principles the Soviet Union had committed itself to in the Helsinki Final Act. Reportedly, the pope's timely letter had a significant effect in dissuading the Soviet Union from intervening with its troops in Poland in 1980, as it had intervened to crush freedom in Prague in 1968 and in Budapest in 1956.

It was true that, at the time, the Soviets were bogged down in an unwinnable war in Afghanistan, and that fact surely weighed heavily in any decision about whether or not to get involved militarily in Poland as well. But the pope's letter may well also have had a significant effect as well. For up to that time maintaining its position in the Communist satellite countries of Eastern Europe had been an unshakable imperative of Soviet policy. The pope was going up against great odds in deciding to write his letter to Brezhnev.

Much has since been written and said about how the election of a pope from behind the Iron Curtain ultimately helped bring about the fall of Soviet Communism at the end of the same decade of the 1980s. There can be no doubt that there is a great deal of truth in this assertion; but it is also evident from this case that Pope John Paul II was already heavily engaged in the area from the time of his election on, and *Dignitatis Humanae* provided him with one of the chief motives and sources and justifications for all his actions in this regard. It should not be imagined that words in documents never have any applications in the real world.

Moreover, the principles articulated in this particular Declaration have proved to be enormously important in the post-conciliar era generally. No doubt they will continue to be equally or more important in the future. This is true, of course, of many documents issued by the Second Vatican Council, but it is especially true of this Declaration with which we have been concerned in this book. The document can only grow in importance, given the problems that confront both the Church and the world today — problems that range from the so-called "clash of civilizations," through the current bio-technological revolution, to the increasing secularization (and growing depopulation) of what was formerly Christendom.

There also presses upon us the continuing threat of so-called "totalitarian democracy," along with the continuing, unrelenting pressures in our society from those who deny truth, or, worse, who are determined to set up false or ersatz "truths" in its place (and are only too often successful in doing so!). In the midst of all of this, there thus remains the ever present necessity for all of us — working out in freedom our "own salvation with fear and trembling" (Phil 2:12). In that important and indeed essential enterprise, Vatican Council II's Declaration on Religious Freedom, *Dignitatis Humanae*, provides us with some important — and true! — principles and guidelines which we should not hesitate to call upon and use in the course of our participation in the Church's continuing earthly pilgrimage. We should never forget what this document teaches us, namely, that the Catholic Church *is* "the teacher of truth." For we cannot remind ourselves too often that it was none other than Jesus Christ himself who taught us that "you will know the truth, and the truth will make you free" (Jn 8:32).

Vatican Council II
Declaration on Religious Freedom
Dignitatis Humanae
On the Right of the Person and of Communities
to Social and Civil Freedom in Matters Religious

Promulgated by His Holiness Pope Paul VI on December 7, 1965

1. A sense of the dignity of the human person has been impressing itself more and more deeply on the consciousness of contemporary man,[1] and the demand is increasingly made that men should act on their own judgment, enjoying and making use of a responsible freedom, not driven by coercion but motivated by a sense of duty. The demand is likewise made that constitutional limits should be set to the powers of government, in order that there may be no encroachment on the rightful freedom of the person and of associations. This demand for freedom in human society chiefly regards the quest for the values proper to the human spirit. It regards, in the first place, the free exercise of religion in society. This Vatican Council takes careful note of these desires in the minds of men. It proposes to declare them to be greatly in accord with truth and justice. To this end, it searches into the sacred tradition and doctrine of the Church — the treasury out of which the Church continually brings forth new things that are in harmony with the things that are old.

First, the Council professes its belief that God Himself has made known to mankind the way in which men are to serve Him, and thus be saved in Christ and come to blessedness. We believe that this one true religion subsists in the Catholic and Apostolic Church, to which the Lord Jesus committed the duty of spreading it abroad among all men. Thus He spoke to the Apostles: "Go, therefore, and make disciples of all nations, baptizing them in the name of the Father and of the Son and of the Holy Spirit, teaching them to observe all things whatsoever I have enjoined upon you" (Mt 28:19-20). On their part, all men are bound to seek the truth, especially in what concerns God and His Church, and to embrace the truth they come to know, and to hold fast to it.

This Vatican Council likewise professes its belief that it is upon the human conscience that these obligations fall and exert their binding force. The truth cannot impose itself except by virtue of its own truth, as it makes its entrance into the mind at once quietly and with power.

Religious freedom, in turn, which men demand as necessary to fulfill their duty to worship God, has to do with immunity from coercion in civil society. Therefore it leaves untouched traditional Catholic doctrine on the moral duty of men and societies toward the true religion and toward the one Church of Christ.

Chapter I: The General Principle of Religious Freedom

Over and above all this, the Council intends to develop the doctrine of recent popes on the inviolable rights of the human person and the constitutional order of society.

2. This Vatican Council declares that the human person has a right to religious freedom. This freedom means that all men are to be immune from coercion on the part of individuals or of social groups and of any human power, in such wise that no one is to be forced to act in a manner contrary to his own beliefs, whether

privately or publicly, whether alone or in association with others, within due limits.

The Council further declares that the right to religious freedom has its foundation in the very dignity of the human person as this dignity is known through the revealed word of God and by reason itself.[2] This right of the human person to religious freedom is to be recognized in the constitutional law whereby society is governed and thus it is to become a civil right.

It is in accordance with their dignity as persons — that is, beings endowed with reason and free will and therefore privileged to bear personal responsibility — that all men should be at once impelled by nature and also bound by a moral obligation to seek the truth, especially religious truth. They are also bound to adhere to the truth, once it is known, and to order their whole lives in accord with the demands of truth. However, men cannot discharge these obligations in a manner in keeping with their own nature unless they enjoy immunity from external coercion as well as psychological freedom. Therefore the right to religious freedom has its foundation not in the subjective disposition of the person, but in his very nature. In consequence, the right to this immunity continues to exist even in those who do not live up to their obligation of seeking the truth and adhering to it and the exercise of this right is not to be impeded, provided that just public order is observed.

3. Further light is shed on the subject if one considers that the highest norm of human life is the divine law — eternal, objective and universal — whereby God orders, directs and governs the entire universe and all the ways of the human community by a plan conceived in wisdom and love. Man has been made by God to participate in this law, with the result that, under the gentle disposition of divine Providence, he can come to perceive ever more fully the truth that is unchanging. Wherefore every man has the duty, and therefore the right, to seek the truth in matters religious in order that he may with prudence form for himself right and true

judgments of conscience, under use of all suitable means.

Truth, however, is to be sought after in a manner proper to the dignity of the human person and his social nature. The inquiry is to be free, carried on with the aid of teaching or instruction, communication and dialogue, in the course of which men explain to one another the truth they have discovered, or think they have discovered, in order thus to assist one another in the quest for truth.

Moreover, as the truth is discovered, it is by a personal assent that men are to adhere to it.

On his part, man perceives and acknowledges the imperatives of the divine law through the mediation of conscience. In all his activity a man is bound to follow his conscience in order that he may come to God, the end and purpose of life. It follows that he is not to be forced to act in manner contrary to his conscience. Nor, on the other hand, is he to be restrained from acting in accordance with his conscience, especially in matters religious. The reason is that the exercise of religion, of its very nature, consists before all else in those internal, voluntary and free acts whereby man sets the course of his life directly toward God. No merely human power can either command or prohibit acts of this kind.[3] The social nature of man, however, itself requires that he should give external expression to his internal acts of religion: that he should share with others in matters religious; that he should profess his religion in community. Injury therefore is done to the human person and to the very order established by God for human life, if the free exercise of religion is denied in society, provided just public order is observed.

There is a further consideration. The religious acts whereby men, in private and in public and out of a sense of personal conviction, direct their lives to God transcend by their very nature the order of terrestrial and temporal affairs. Government therefore ought indeed to take account of the religious life of the citizenry and show it favor, since the function of government is to make provision for the common welfare. However, it would clearly transgress the limits set to its power, were it to presume to command or inhibit acts that are religious.

4. The freedom or immunity from coercion in matters religious which is the endowment of persons as individuals is also to be recognized as their right when they act in community. Religious communities are a requirement of the social nature both of man and of religion itself.

Provided the just demands of public order are observed, religious communities rightfully claim freedom in order that they may govern themselves according to their own norms, honor the Supreme Being in public worship, assist their members in the practice of the religious life, strengthen them by instruction, and promote institutions in which they may join together for the purpose of ordering their own lives in accordance with their religious principles.

Religious communities also have the right not to be hindered, either by legal measures or by administrative action on the part of government, in the selection, training, appointment, and transfer of their own ministers, in communicating with religious authorities and communities abroad, in erecting buildings for religious purposes, and in the acquisition and use of suitable funds or properties.

Religious communities also have the right not to be hindered in their public teaching and witness to their faith, whether by the spoken or by the written word. However, in spreading religious faith and in introducing religious practices everyone ought at all times to refrain from any manner of action which might seem to carry a hint of coercion or of a kind of persuasion that would be dishonorable or unworthy, especially when dealing with poor or uneducated people. Such a manner of action would have to be considered an abuse of one's right and a violation of the right of others.

In addition, it comes within the meaning of religious freedom that religious communities should not be prohibited from freely undertaking to show the special value of their doctrine in what concerns the organization of society and the inspiration of the whole of human activity. Finally, the social nature of man and the very nature of religion afford the foundation of the right of men freely to hold meetings and to establish educational, cultural, charitable and social organizations, under the impulse of their own religious sense.

5. The family, since it is a society in its own original right, has the right freely to live its own domestic religious life under the guidance of parents. Parents, moreover, have the right to determine, in accordance with their own religious beliefs, the kind of religious education that their children are to receive. Government, in consequence, must acknowledge the right of parents to make a genuinely free choice of schools and of other means of education, and the use of this freedom of choice is not to be made a reason for imposing unjust burdens on parents, whether directly or indirectly. Besides, the rights of parents are violated, if their children are forced to attend lessons or instructions which are not in agreement with their religious beliefs, or if a single system of education, from which all religious formation is excluded, is imposed upon all.

6. Since the common welfare of society consists in the entirety of those conditions of social life under which men enjoy the possibility of achieving their own perfection in a certain fullness of measure and also with some relative ease, it chiefly consists in the protection of the rights, and in the performance of the duties, of the human person.[4] Therefore the care of the right to religious freedom devolves upon the whole citizenry, upon social groups, upon government, and upon the Church and other religious communities, in virtue of the duty of all toward the common welfare, and in the manner proper to each.

The protection and promotion of the inviolable rights of man rank among the essential duties of government.[5] Therefore government is to assume the safeguard of the religious freedom of all its citizens, in an effective manner, by just laws and by other appropriate means.

Government is also to help create conditions favorable to the fostering of religious life, in order that the people may be truly enabled to exercise their religious rights and to fulfill their religious duties, and also in order that society itself may profit by the moral qualities of justice and peace which have their origin in men's faithfulness to God and to His holy will.[6]

If, in view of peculiar circumstances obtaining among peoples, special civil recognition is given to one religious community in the constitutional order of society, it is at the same time imperative that the right of all citizens and religious communities to religious freedom should be recognized and made effective in practice.

Finally, government is to see to it that equality of citizens before the law, which is itself an element of the common good, is never violated, whether openly or covertly, for religious reasons. Nor is there to be discrimination among citizens.

It follows that a wrong is done when government imposes upon its people, by force or fear or other means, the profession or repudiation of any religion, or when it hinders men from joining or leaving a religious community. All the more is it a violation of the will of God and of the sacred rights of the person and the family of nations when force is brought to bear in any way in order to destroy or repress religion, either in the whole of mankind or in a particular country or in a definite community.

7. The right to religious freedom is exercised in human society: hence its exercise is subject to certain regulatory norms. In the use of all freedoms the moral principle of personal and social responsibility is to be observed. In the exercise of their rights, individual men and social groups are bound by the moral law to have respect both for the rights of others and for their own duties toward others and for the common welfare of all. Men are to deal

with their fellows in justice and civility.

Furthermore, society has the right to defend itself against possible abuses committed on the pretext of freedom of religion. It is the special duty of government to provide this protection. However, government is not to act in an arbitrary fashion or in an unfair spirit of partisanship. Its action is to be controlled by juridical norms which are in conformity with the objective moral order. These norms arise out of the need for the effective safeguard of the rights of all citizens and for the peaceful settlement of conflicts of rights, also out of the need for an adequate care of genuine public peace, which comes about when men live together in good order and in true justice, and finally out of the need for a proper guardianship of public morality.

These matters constitute the basic component of the common welfare: they are what is meant by public order. For the rest, the usages of society are to be the usages of freedom in their full range: that is, the freedom of man is to be respected as far as possible and is not to be curtailed except when and insofar as necessary.

8. Many pressures are brought to bear upon the men of our day, to the point where the danger arises lest they lose the possibility of acting on their own judgment. On the other hand, not a few can be found who seem inclined to use the name of freedom as the pretext for refusing to submit to authority and for making light of the duty of obedience. Wherefore this Vatican Council urges everyone, especially those who are charged with the task of educating others, to do their utmost to form men who, on the one hand, will respect the moral order and be obedient to lawful authority, and on the other hand, will be lovers of true freedom — men, in other words, who will come to decisions on their own judgment and in the light of truth, govern their activities with a sense of responsibility, and strive after what is true and right, willing always to join with others in cooperative effort.

Religious freedom therefore ought to have this further

purpose and aim, namely, that men may come to act with greater responsibility in fulfilling their duties in community life.

Chapter II: Religious Freedom in the Light of Revelation

9. The declaration of this Vatican Council on the right of man to religious freedom has its foundation in the dignity of the person, whose exigencies have come to be fully known to human reason through centuries of experience. What is more, this doctrine of freedom has roots in divine revelation, and for this reason Christians are bound to respect it all the more conscientiously. Revelation does not indeed affirm in so many words the right of man to immunity from external coercion in matters religious. It does, however, disclose the dignity of the human person in its full dimensions. It gives evidence of the respect which Christ showed toward the freedom with which man is to fulfill his duty of belief in the word of God and it gives us lessons in the spirit which disciples of such a Master ought to adopt and continually follow. Thus further light is cast upon the general principles upon which the doctrine of this declaration on religious freedom is based. In particular, religious freedom in society is entirely consonant with the freedom of the act of Christian faith.

10. It is one of the major tenets of Catholic doctrine that man's response to God in faith must be free: no one therefore is to be forced to embrace the Christian faith against his own will.[7] This doctrine is contained in the word of God and it was constantly proclaimed by the Fathers of the Church.[8] The act of faith is of its very nature a free act. Man, redeemed by Christ the Savior and through Christ Jesus called to be God's adopted son,[9] cannot give his adherence to God revealing Himself unless, under the drawing of the Father,[10] he offers to God the reasonable and free submission of faith. It is therefore completely in accord with the nature of faith that in matters religious every manner of coercion on the

part of men should be excluded. In consequence, the principle of religious freedom makes no small contribution to the creation of an environment in which men can without hindrance be invited to the Christian faith, embrace it of their own free will, and profess it effectively in their whole manner of life.

11. God calls men to serve Him in spirit and in truth, hence they are bound in conscience but they stand under no compulsion. God has regard for the dignity of the human person whom He Himself created and man is to be guided by his own judgment and he is to enjoy freedom. This truth appears at its height in Christ Jesus, in whom God manifested Himself and His ways with men. Christ is at once our Master and our Lord[11] and also meek and humble of heart.[12] In attracting and inviting His disciples He used patience.[13] He wrought miracles to illuminate His teaching and to establish its truth, but His intention was to rouse faith in His hearers and to confirm them in faith, not to exert coercion upon them.[14] He did indeed denounce the unbelief of some who listened to Him, but He left vengeance to God in expectation of the Day of Judgment.[15] When He sent His Apostles into the world, He said to them: "He who believes and is baptized will be saved. He who does not believe will be condemned" (Mk 16:16). But He Himself, noting that the cockle had been sown amid the wheat, gave orders that both should be allowed to grow until the harvest time, which will come at the end of the world.[16] He refused to be a political messiah, ruling by force:[17] He preferred to call Himself the Son of Man, who came "to serve and to give his life as a ransom for the many" (Mk 10:45). He showed Himself the perfect servant of God,[18] who "does not break the bruised reed nor extinguish the smoking flax" (Mt 12:20).

He acknowledged the power of government and its rights, when He commanded that tribute be given to Caesar: but He gave clear warning that the higher rights of God are to be kept inviolate: "Render to Caesar the things that are Caesar's and to God the things that are God's" (Mt 22:21). In the end, when He completed on the cross the work of redemption whereby He achieved salvation and true freedom for men, He brought His revelation to completion. He bore witness to the truth,[19] but He refused to impose the truth by force on those who spoke against it. Not by force of blows does His rule assert its claims.[20] It is established by witnessing to the truth and by hearing the truth, and it extends its dominion by the love whereby Christ, lifted up on the cross, draws all men to Himself.[21]

Taught by the word and example of Christ, the Apostles followed the same way. From the very origins of the Church the disciples of Christ strove to convert men to faith in Christ as the Lord; not, however, by the use of coercion or of devices unworthy of the Gospel, but by the power, above all, of the word of God.[22] Steadfastly they proclaimed to all the plan of God our Savior, "who wills that all men should be saved and come to the acknowledgment of the truth" (1 Tm 2:4). At the same time, however, they showed respect for those of weaker stuff, even though they were in error, and thus they made it plain that "each one of us is to render to God an account of himself" (Rm 14:12),[23] and for that reason is bound to obey his conscience. Like Christ Himself, the Apostles were unceasingly bent upon bearing witness to the truth of God, and they showed the fullest measure of boldness in "speaking the word with confidence" (Ac 4:31)[24] before the people and their rulers. With a firm faith they held that the Gospel is indeed the power of God unto salvation for all who believe.[25] Therefore they rejected all "carnal weapons";[26] they followed the example of the gentleness and respectfulness of Christ and they preached the word of God in the full confidence that there was resident in this word itself a divine power able to destroy all the forces arrayed against God[27] and bring men to faith in Christ and to His service.[28] As the Master, so too the Apostles recognized legitimate civil authority. "For there is no power except from God," the Apostle teaches, and thereafter commands: "Let everyone be subject to higher authorities.... He who resists authority resists God's ordinance" (Rm 13:1-5).[29] At the same time, however, they did not hesitate to speak out against governing powers which set themselves in opposition to the holy will of God: "It is necessary to obey God rather than men" (Ac 5:29).[30] This is the way along which the martyrs and other faithful have walked through all ages and over all the earth.

12. In faithfulness therefore to the truth of the Gospel, the Church is following the way of Christ and the Apostles when she recognizes and gives support to the principle of religious freedom as befitting the dignity of man and as being in accord with divine revelation. Throughout the ages the Church has kept safe and handed on the doctrine received from the Master and from the Apostles. In the life of the People of God, as it has made its pilgrim way through the vicissitudes of human history, there has at times appeared a way of acting that was hardly in accord with the spirit of the Gospel or even opposed to it. Nevertheless, the doctrine of the Church that no one is to be coerced into faith has always stood firm.

Thus the leaven of the Gospel has long been about its quiet work in the minds of men, and to it is due in great measure the fact that in the course of time men have come more widely to recognize their dignity as persons, and the conviction has grown stronger that the person in society is to be kept free from all manner of coercion in matters religious.

13. Among the things that concern the good of the Church and indeed the welfare of society here on earth — things therefore that are always and everywhere to be kept secure and defended against all injury — this certainly is preeminent, namely, that the Church should enjoy that full measure of freedom which her care for the salvation of men requires.[31] This is a sacred freedom, because the only-begotten Son endowed with it the Church which He purchased with His blood. Indeed it is so much the property of

the Church that to act against it is to act against the will of God. The freedom of the Church is the fundamental principle in what concerns the relations between the Church and governments and the whole civil order.

In human society and in the face of government the Church claims freedom for herself in her character as a spiritual authority, established by Christ the Lord, upon which there rests, by divine mandate, the duty of going out into the whole world and preaching the Gospel to every creature.[32] The Church also claims freedom for herself in her character as a society of men who have the right to live in society in accordance with the precepts of the Christian faith.[33]

In turn, where the principle of religious freedom is not only proclaimed in words or simply incorporated in law but also given sincere and practical application, there the Church succeeds in achieving a stable situation of right as well as of fact and the independence which is necessary for the fulfillment of her divine mission.

This independence is precisely what the authorities of the Church claim in society.[34] At the same time, the Christian faithful, in common with all other men, possess the civil right not to be hindered in leading their lives in accordance with their consciences. Therefore, a harmony exists between the freedom of the Church and the religious freedom which is to be recognized as the right of all men and communities and sanctioned by constitutional law.

14. In order to be faithful to the divine command, "teach all nations" (Mt 28:19-20), the Catholic Church must work with all urgency and concern "that the word of God be spread abroad and glorified" (2 Th 3:1). Hence the Church earnestly begs of its children that, "first of all, supplications, prayers, petitions, acts of thanksgiving be made for all men.... For this is good and agreeable in the sight of God our Savior, who wills that all men be saved and come to the knowledge of the truth" (1 Tm 2:1-4). In the formation

of their consciences, the Christian faithful ought carefully to attend to the sacred and certain doctrine of the Church.[35] For the Church is, by the will of Christ, the teacher of the truth. It is her duty to give utterance to, and authoritatively to teach, that truth which is Christ Himself, and also to declare and confirm by her authority those principles of the moral order which have their origins in human nature itself. Furthermore, let Christians walk in wisdom in the face of those outside, "in the Holy Spirit, in unaffected love, in the word of truth" (2 Cor 6:6-7), and let them be about their task of spreading the light of life with all confidence[36] and apostolic courage, even to the shedding of their blood.

The disciple is bound by a grave obligation toward Christ, his Master, ever more fully to understand the truth received from Him, faithfully to proclaim it, and vigorously to defend it, never — be it understood — having recourse to means that are incompatible with the spirit of the Gospel. At the same time, the charity of Christ urges him to love and have prudence and patience in his dealings with those who are in error or in ignorance with regard to the faith.[37] All is to be taken into account — the Christian duty to Christ, the life-giving word which must be proclaimed, the rights of the human person, and the measure of grace granted by God through Christ to men who are invited freely to accept and profess the faith.

15. The fact is that men of the present day want to be able freely to profess their religion in private and in public. Indeed, religious freedom has already been declared to be a civil right in most constitutions, and it is solemnly recognized in international documents.[38] The further fact is that forms of government still exist under which, even though freedom of religious worship receives constitutional recognition, the powers of government are engaged in the effort to deter citizens from the profession of religion and to make life very difficult and dangerous for religious communities.

This council greets with joy the first of these two facts as among the signs of the times. With sorrow, however, it denounces the other fact, as only to be deplored. The council exhorts Catholics, and it directs a plea to all men, most carefully to consider how greatly necessary religious freedom is, especially in the present condition of the human family. All nations are coming into even closer unity. Men of different cultures and religions are being brought together in closer relationships. There is a growing consciousness of the personal responsibility that every man has. All this is evident. Consequently, in order that relationships of peace and harmony be established and maintained within the whole of mankind, it is necessary that religious freedom be everywhere provided with an effective constitutional guarantee and that respect be shown for the high duty and right of man freely to lead his religious life in society.

May the God and Father of all grant that the human family, through careful observance of the principle of religious freedom in society, may be brought by the grace of Christ and the power of the Holy Spirit to the sublime and unending and "glorious freedom of the sons of God" (Rm 8:21).

(The above text is the Vatican translation taken from the Vatican website: www.vatican.va)

Footnotes

[1] Cf. John XXIII, encycl. *Pacem in Terris*, April 11, 1963: AAS (1963) p. 279; *ibid.*, p. 265; Pius XII, radio message, Dec. 24, 1944: AAS 37 (1945), p. 14.

[2] Cf. John XXIII, encycl. *Pacem in Terris*, April 11, 1963: AAS 55 (1963), pp. 260-261; Pius XII, radio message, Dec. 24, 1942: AAS 35 (1943), p. 19; Pius XI, encycl. *Mit Brennender Sorge*, March 14, 1937: AAS 29 (1937), p. 160; Leo XIII, encycl. *Libertas Praestantissimum*, June 20, 1888: Acts of Leo XIII 8 (1888), p. 237-238.

[3] Cf. John XXIII, encycl. *Pacem in Terris*, April 11, 1963: AAS 55 (1963), p. 270; Paul VI, radio message, Dec. 22, 1964: AAS 57 (1965), pp. 181-182.

[4] Cf. John XXIII, encycl. *Mater et Magistra*, May 15, 1961: AAS 53 (1961), p. 417; idem, encycl. *Pacem in Terris*, April 11, 1963: AAS 55 (1963), p. 273.

5 Cf. John XXIII, encycl. *Pacem in Terris*, April 11, 1963: AAS 55 (1963), pp. 273-274; Pius XII, radio message, June 1 1941: AAS 33 (1941), p. 200.

6 Cf. Leo XIII, encycl. *Immortale Dei*, Nov. 1, 1885: AAS 18 (1885) p. 161.

7 Cf. CIC, c. *1351*; Pius XII, *allocution to prelate auditors and other officials and administrators of the tribune of the Holy Roman Rota*, Oct. 6, 1946: AAS 38 (1946), p. 394; idem. Encycl. *Mystici Corporis*, June 29, 1943: AAS (1943) p. 243.

8 Cf. Lactantius, *Divinarum Institutionum*, Book V, 19: CSEL 19, pp. 463-464, 465: PL 6, 614 and 616 (ch. 20); St. Ambrose, *Epistola ad Valentianum Imp.*, Letter 21: PL 16, 1005; St. Augustine, *Contra Litteras Petiliani*, Book II, ch. 83: CSEL 52 p. 112: PL 43, 315; cf. C. 23, q. 5, c. 33, (ed. Friedberg, col. 939); idem, Letter 23: PL 33, 98, idem, Letter 34: PL 33, 132; idem, Letter 35: PL 33, 135; St. Gregory the Great, *Epistola ad Virgilium et Theodorum Episcopos Massiliae Galliarum*, Register of Letters I, 45: MGH Ep. 1, p. 72: PL 77, 510-511 (Book I, ep. 47); idem, *Epistola ad Johannem Episcopum Constantinopolitanum*, Register of Letters, III, 52: MGH Letter 1, p. 210: PL 77, 649 (Book III, Letter 53); cf. D. 45, c. 1 (ed. Friedberg, col 160); Council of Toledo IV, c. 57: Mansi 10, 633; cf. D. 45, c. 5 (ed. Friedberg, col. 161-162); Clement III: X., V, 6, 9: ed. Friedberg, col. 774; Innocent III, *Epistola ad Arelatensem Archiepiscopum*, X, III, 42, 3: Friedberg, col. 646.

9 Cf. Eph 1:5.

10 Cf. Jn 6:44.

11 Cf. Jn 13:13.

12 Cf. Mt 11:29.

13 Cf. Mt 11:28-30; Jn 6:67-68.

14 Cf. Mt 9:28-29; Mk 9:23-24; 6:5-6; Paul VI, encycl. *Ecclesiam Suam*, Aug. 6, 1964: AAS 56 (1964), pp. 642-643.

15 Cf. Mt 11:20-24; Rm 12:19-20; 2 Th 1:8.

16 Cf. Mt 13:30 and 40-42.

17 Cf. Mt 4:8-10; Jn 6:15.

18 Cf. Is 42:1-4.

19 Cf. Jn 18:37.

20 Cf. Mt 26:51-53; Jn 18:36.

21 Cf. Jn 12:32.

22 Cf. 1 Cor 2:3-5; 1 Th 2:3-5.

23 Cf. Rm 14:1-23; 1 Cor 8:9-13; 10:23-33.

24 Cf. Eph 6:19-20.

25 Cf. Rm 1:16.

26 Cf. 2 Cor 10:4; 1 Th 5:8-9.

27 Cf. Eph 6:11-17.

28 Cf. 2 Cor 10:3-5.

[29] Cf. 1 P 2:13-17.

[30] Cf. Ac 4: 19-20.

[31] Cf. Leo XIII, letter *Officio Sanctissimo*, Dec. 22 1887: AAS 20 (1887), p. 269; idem., letter "Ex Litteris," April 7 1887: AAS 19 (1886), p. 465.

[32] Cf. Mk 16:15; Mt 28:18-20, Pius XII, encycl. *Summi Pontificatus*, Oct. 20, 1939: AAS 31 (1939). pp. 445-446.

[33] Cf. Pius XI, letter *Firmissimam Constantiam*, March 28, 1937: AAS 29 (1937), p. 196.

[34] Cf. Pius XII, allocution, "Ci Riesce," Dec. 6, 1953: AAS 45 (1953), p. 802.

[35] Cf. Pius XII, radio message, March 23, 1952: AAS 44 (1952) pp. 270-278.

[36] Cf. Ac 4:29.

[37] Cf. John XXIII, encycl. *Pacem in Terris*, April 11, 1963: AAS 55 (1963), pp. 299-300.

[38] Cf. John XXIII, encycl. *Pacem in Terris*, April 11, 1963:AAS 55 (1963) pp. 295-296.

SELECTED BIBLIOGRAPHY

Abbott, Walter M., SJ, General Editor, *The Documents of Vatican II* (New York: Herder and Herder/Association Press, 1966).

Bevins, Stephen B., SVD, and Jeffrey Gros, FSC, *Evangelization and Religious Freedom: Ad Gentes, Dignitatis Humanae* (New York/Mahwah, NJ: Paulist Press, 2009).

Bunson, Matthew, General Editor, *2009 Catholic Almanac* (Huntington, IN: Our Sunday Visitor Publishing Division, 2009) and similar volumes from previous years.

Carlin, Claudia, IHM, Editor, *The Papal Encyclicals – 1740-1981* [5 Volumes] (Raleigh, NC: McGrath Publishing Company, 1981).

D'Arcy, Eric, *Conscience and Its Right to Freedom* (New York: Sheed and Ward, 1961).

D'Elia, Donald J. and Stephen M. Krason, Editors, *We Hold These Truths and More: Further Catholic Reflections on the American Proposition* (Steubenville, OH: Franciscan University Press, 1993).

Farr, Thomas F., *World of Faith and Freedom: Why International Religious Liberty is Vital to American National Security* (Oxford/New York: Oxford University Press, 2008).

Fesquet, Henri, *The Drama of Vatican II: The Ecumenical Council June, 1962-December, 1965* (New York: Random House, 1967).

Flannery, Austin, OP, General Editor, *Vatican Council II: The Conciliar and Post-Conciliar Documents* (Northport, NY: Costello Publishing Company, 1975).

Grasso, Kenneth L. and Robert P. Hunt, Editors, *Catholicism and Religious Freedom: Contemporary Reflections on Vatican II's Declaration on Religious Liberty* (Lanham, MD: Rowman & Littlefield Publishers, Inc., 2006).

Hebblethwaite, Peter, *Pope John XXIII: Shepherd of the Modern World* (New York: Doubleday and Company, 1985).

_____. *Paul VI: The First Modern Pope* (New York/Mahwah, NJ: Paulist Press, 1993).

John XXIII, Pope, Encyclical Letter on Peace on Earth, *Pacem in Terris*, April 11, 1963 (Boston, MA: Daughters of St. Paul, 1963).

John Paul II, Pope, Encyclical Letter on the Redeemer of Man, *Redemptor Hominis,* March 4, 1979, (Washington, DC: U.S. Catholic Conference Publications Office, 1979).

_____. "Letter on Negotiation: The Only Realistic Solution to the Continuing Threat of War," June 11, 1982 (Boston, MA: Daughters of St. Paul, 1982).

Küng, Hans, Yves Congar, OP, and David O'Hanlon, SJ, Editors, *Council Speeches of Vatican II* (Glen Rock, NJ: Paulist Press, 1964).

McInerny, Ralph, Editor, *Catholic Dossier* Issue on *Dignitatis Humanae* (Vol. 6, No. 2, March-April, 2000).

Murray, John Courtney, SJ, *We Hold These Truths: Catholic Reflections on the American Proposition* (New York: Sheed and Ward, 1960).

_____. *Religious Liberty: Catholic Struggles with Pluralism.* Edited by J. Leon Hooper, SJ (Louisville, KY: Westminster/ John Knox Press, 1993).

Paul VI, Pope, Encyclical Letter on the Paths of the Church, *Ecclesiam Suam* (Boston: St. Paul Editions, 1964).

Prendergast, Michael R., and M.D. Ridge, *Voices from the Council* (Portland: Pastoral Press, 2004).

Ratzinger, Cardinal Joseph (with Vittorio Messori), *The Ratzinger Report: An Exclusive Interview on the State of the Church* (San Francisco: Ignatius Press, 1985).

_____. *Church, Ecumenism & Politics: New Essays in Ecclesiology* (New York: Crossroad Books, 1987).

Rynne, Xavier, *Vatican Council II* (New York: Farrar, Straus and Giroux, 1968).

Stacpoole, Alberic, OSB, Editor, *Vatican II Revisited: By Those Who Were There* (Minneapolis: Winston Press, 1986).

Whitehead, Kenneth D., *The New Ecumenism: How the Catholic Church After Vatican II Took Over the Leadership of the World Ecumenical Movement* (Staten Island, NY: ST PAULS / Alba House, 2009).

Wiltgen, Rev. Ralph M., SVD, *The Rhine Flows into the Tiber: The Unknown Council* (New York: Hawthorn Books, Inc., 1967).

ABOUT THE AUTHOR

Kenneth D. Whitehead is a former career Foreign Service Officer who served in Rome, the Middle East, and North Africa, but later completed his federal government career in the U.S. Department of Education as President Ronald Reagan's Assistant Secretary of Education for Post-secondary Education. He now works as a writer, editor, and translator in Falls Church, Virginia. He is the author, among other books, of *One, Holy, Catholic, and Apostolic: The Early Church Was the Catholic Church* (Ignatius Press, 2000), and, most recently, *The New Ecumenism: How the Catholic Church after Vatican II Took over the Leadership of the World Ecumenical Movement* (ST PAULS/Alba House, 2009). He is the co-author (with James Likoudis) of *The Pope, the Council, and the Mass* (Revised Edition, Emmaus Road Publishing, 2006). He has authored, co-authored, edited, or translated a number of other books, mostly of Catholic interest, including *The Church, Marriage, and the Family* (St. Augustine's Press, 2007), and he has translated Archbishop Agostino Marchetto's *Il Concilio Ecumenico Vaticano II* (*The Second Vatican Ecumenical Council: A Counterpoint for the History of the Council*, University of Scranton Press [dist. by the University of Chicago Press], 2010).

Mr. Whitehead was educated at the University of Utah and the University of Paris, and holds an honorary D.Litt. Degree in Christian Letters from the Franciscan University of Steubenville. He serves on the Boards of Directors of the Catholic League for Religious and Civil Rights, the Fellowship of Catholic Scholars, and the *Review of Metaphysics*. Mr. Whitehead is married to the former Margaret O'Donohue, long a parish director of religious education, and they are the parents of four grown sons.